D1611808

Dwight F. Burlingame, Timothy L. Seiler,
Eugene R. Tempel
Indiana University Center on Philanthropy
EDITORS

UNDERSTANDING AND IMPROVING THE LANGUAGE OF FUNDRAISING

Timothy L. Seiler
Indiana University Center on Philanthropy

EDITOR

NUMBER 22, WINTER 1998

UNDERSTANDING AND IMPROVING THE LANGUAGE OF FUNDRAISING
Timothy L. Seiler (ed.)
New Directions for Philanthropic Fundraising, No. 22, Winter 1998
Dwight F. Burlingame, Timothy L. Seiler, Eugene R. Tempel, Editors

NEW DIRECTIONS FOR PHILANTHROPIC FUNDRAISING is indexed in Higher Education
Abstracts and Philanthropic Index.

Microfilm copies of issues and articles are available in 16 mm and 35 mm, as well as
microfiche in 105 mm, through University Microfilms Inc., 300 North Zeeb Road,
Ann Arbor, Michigan 48106-1346.

ISSN 1072-172X   ISBN 0-7879-4863-2

NEW DIRECTIONS FOR PHILANTHROPIC FUNDRAISING is part of The Jossey-Bass
Nonprofit Sector Series and is published quarterly by Jossey-Bass Inc., Publishers,
350 Sansome Street, San Francisco, California 94104-1342.

SUBSCRIPTIONS cost $67.00 for individuals and $115.00 for institutions, agencies, and
libraries. Prices subject to change. Refer to the Ordering Information page at the back
of this issue.

EDITORIAL CORRESPONDENCE should be sent to the editor, Dwight F. Burlingame,
Center on Philanthropy, Indiana University, 550 West North Street, Suite 301,
Indianapolis, IN 46202-3162.

www.josseybass.com

Printed in the United States of America on acid-free recycled paper containing 100
percent recovered waste paper, of which at least 20 percent is postconsumer waste.

Contents

Editor's Notes

THE CHAPTERS IN THIS VOLUME were originally papers developed for presentation at a symposium on the language of fundraising. This symposium is an annual event sponsored by the Indiana University Center on Philanthropy with the purpose of bringing together academic scholars and fundraising practitioners. The eleventh annual symposium, "Language and Rhetoric of Fundraising," was held in Indianapolis in August 1998. Nearly two hundred fundraising practitioners and scholars of linguistics and rhetoric convened for two days to share ideas about how language is used in fundraising as they analyzed and discussed a range of fundraising pieces, including direct mail letters, grant proposals, capital campaign brochures, annual reports, and even Web sites. This volume represents a sampling of the papers presented at the symposium by groups of scholars and practitioners that were subsequently revised and edited for this publication.

The papers at the symposium, and the chapters in this volume, are probably an accurate reflection of the state of fundraising today: the emphasis is on written language—direct mail and grant proposals, for example—with an acknowledgment that visual language is also important. Only one chapter in this volume treats visual rhetoric.

Despite the limitations of such a "conventional" approach to language, this volume offers helpful and practical analyses of how language is used in fundraising appeals. For scholars, this seems to open new territories for scholarly research. For fundraisers, it challenges an awareness of language from a different perspective: that of the linguist who analyzes language for its effects. Reading these

NEW DIRECTIONS FOR PHILANTHROPIC FUNDRAISING, NO. 22, WINTER 1998 © JOSSEY-BASS PUBLISHERS

chapters offers a thoughtful approach and a sensitivity to how language works in fundraising.

Charles Bazerman's work appears at first glance to be another case study of how fundraising is a values exchange between the giver (donor) and the nonprofit organization. Nothing new here for the practitioner. But there's far more in this chapter: a fascinating retelling of how a nonprofit moves from grant dependency to a fully developed fundraising organization. Although Bazerman focuses on how volunteering leads to giving, which leads to community building, the chapter has the side benefit of tracing how boards become actively engaged as givers and askers, and how fundraisers professionalize themselves and the fundraising process. Bazerman's recounting of a specific fundraising project is a compelling opening to the idea of how the personal benefit of giving combines with a community sense of pride, even moral commitment.

A fundraising practitioner, Donald N. Ritzenhein contributes a rigorous analysis of the various arguments fundraisers use in direct mail. Ritzenhein challenges the rather commonly held notion of fundraising as an exchange of values. His content analysis of direct mail letters reveals a wide range of motivations used to encourage the reader to give. His study reports findings to questions ranging from the kinds of arguments used in direct mail letters to the extent these arguments are based on emotional or logical appeals. His conclusions offer hypotheses for further research into what persuades donors to give.

Peter McCagg challenges us to be aware of how widespread the use of metaphor is in everyday language as well as in philanthropic fundraising. He provides several distinctive "kinds" of metaphors along with recognizable examples to demonstrate how readily, and perhaps unthinkingly, we use metaphorical language. McCagg urges an awareness of metaphors so that philanthropic fundraising will use effective and appropriate metaphors in philanthropic discourse. Like Ritzenhein, McCagg challenges scholars and fundraisers to conduct further research into the impact of this linguistic device on donors' responsiveness to fundraising appeals.

The next two chapters take up the analysis of grant proposals—from how the proposal is first written to what additional benefits (besides the money!) accrue to an organization when a proposal is successful through its being funded. Molly Flaherty Haas uses case studies of how proposals are developed. In her chapter, Haas stresses the importance of recognizing the individual nature of each grant proposal. An intriguing notion is the difference between language used in a small grant proposal and in a large grant proposal. Haas uses a functional definition of small and large from the organizations she studied, and her conclusions about what the language reflects in each instance will be of interest to fundraisers and scholars.

Ulla Connor and Lilya Wagner bring together in their chapter the essence of the symposium that prompted the papers that constitute this volume: a scholar and a fundraiser combining their expertise to develop a topic of common interest. The two studied how several nonprofits formulated grant proposals and adapted them to the expectations of potential funders. Their chapter looks at structure, awareness of audience, and presentation of identity in proposals written for Latino nonprofit organizations. Their study is important for the issues it raises about adherence to conventional Anglo expectations by a growing Latino population seeking funds through grant proposals.

The one chapter in the volume that addresses visual rhetoric is Patricia Sullivan's "Into Print, into Webs: The Consideration of Visual Rhetoric for Print and On-Line Philanthropic Documents." Just as nonprofits must be concerned about their printed materials—"We can't look too expensive"—so too the look matters: nonprofits want to create a sense of urgency for their project so that potential funders will want to get onboard. The chapter offers a handy set of pluses and minuses to consider about a nonprofit's Web presence. One of the most helpful elements of Sullivan's chapter is a list of practical questions to ask about print and on-line visual rhetoric. Sullivan shows in this list an understanding of the donor focus necessary for fundraising.

Of all the chapters in this volume, the last comes closest to placing positive value on the act of fundraising and the language used to encourage or promote the act. Vijay K. Bhatia compares the promotional nature of direct mail fundraising letters with the promotional discourse of commercial advertising. Bhatia cites the similarity in communicative purposes and distinguishes the types primarily by describing philanthropic fundraising as "a form of moral action." Even in the increasingly competitive environment for fundraising, argues Bhatia, philanthropic fundraising discourse appropriates a wider range of linguistic strategies to attract donors. Bhatia's chapter describes an important assumption of philanthropic fundraising as the establishment and maintenance of community values. Fundraising's use of a large variety of creative options is seen in a positive light, and Bhatia credits fundraising discourse as a form of language use second in its dynamic nature only to literary genres. Bhatia's chapter, then, serves not just as an end to the volume but also as a more positive perspective of the "good" in fundraising language. His is a view that opens possibilities to the positive side of fundraising language.

In fundraising, too often we take language for granted—we use it carelessly, or worse, thoughtlessly. Even the term *fundraising* itself (although Peter McCagg's chapter on metaphors offers a positive interpretation) has negative connotations, or at least many people have negative associations. How often do people describe fundraising as begging, manipulation, combat, or "hitting up your friends?" With such metaphors associated with fundraising, is it any wonder that board members of nonprofits so often lament that they will do anything but fundraising?

Besides these unpleasant metaphors, note these other commonly used terms: *suspects, prospects, acquisition, campaign, target.* Are these terms wholesome and inviting? Don't they create or at least imply something unsavory? Unfortunately, the language of fundraising is laden with unwholesome and combative terms. It is not uncommon for people to talk about "getting their hands dirty" by doing fundraising.

But there is a positive side to the language of fundraising. We can concentrate on fundraising as mission-centered, making possible program and service delivery. Fundraising lifts an organization, it addresses community needs, solves problems, provides a public benefit.

This volume on the language of fundraising calls us to an awareness of and sensitivity to language and its effect on the users and the hearers (or readers). Scholars and practitioners alike present thoughtful analyses and offer provocative challenges to fundraising to help us understand better how we use language to take fundraising seriously and with pride. This volume is the first step toward the ultimate endorsement of the positive aspects of fundraising: a fundraiser with a thorough knowledge of the mission, dedication to the cause, and no fear of giving or raising money—on the next Oprah.

Timothy L. Seiler
Editor

TIMOTHY L. SEILER *is director of public service and The Fund Raising School at the Indiana University Center on Philanthropy.*

This chapter identifies features of a fundraising appeal that elicited extraordinary giving by tapping into individual commitment during a campaign to preserve a California community's highly valued coastal property.

1

Green giving: Engagement, values, activism, and community life

Charles Bazerman

IN A PREVIOUS STUDY, I observed that fundraising texts engage potential donors by creating social roles and status for the benefactors and by providing values through which they can define themselves. Fundraising documents particularly appeal to the emotions of shame and pride—by representing a social rupture in the need situation (something shameful) and social healing in the act of charity (something one could be proud of). Fundraising, I argued, could increase the psychic and identity rewards of giving by engaging the gift-givers with the work and activity of the charitable organization, and it could reach beyond the limited budget people usually allocate to psychic goods by establishing charitable gifts as part of the costs of their way of life and part of the meanings, activities, and communities within which they live their lives (Bazerman, 1997).

In other words, fundraising documents could provide a variety of psychic rewards in exchange for the potential gift—reinforcing

NEW DIRECTIONS FOR PHILANTHROPIC FUNDRAISING, NO. 22, WINTER 1998 © JOSSEY-BASS PUBLISHERS

givers' sense of social power, allowing them to assert their personal values into a wider sphere or attach themselves to admirable public values, or giving them the opportunity to empathize with social ruptures and perceive themselves proudly as social healers, particularly in relation to the ruptures and healings of their own lives. However, the amount people allotted to such psychic rewards seemed limited to, on average, 2 percent to 3 percent of income (Kelly, 1997). Only when people seemed to see the giving as part of their more general activities, commitments, and communities—like when giving to their religious congregation—would it be more substantial, because it came to be seen as part of the general expenses of their way of life.

Environmentalism in Santa Barbara and community awareness

To explore these ideas more concretely, this chapter examines fundraising in Santa Barbara for environmental causes—causes associated strongly with community values, historical ruptures and healing in the region, continuing activism in the region, and the community's way of life.

Santa Barbara has historically had a sense of itself as an aesthetic and environmentally planned community. The city has been a major tourist destination and home to a substantial population of the wealthy and famous since at least 1875. When oil development came around the turn of the century, strong community opposition to unrestrained development led to resistance and regulation (Molotch, Freudenburg, and Paulsen, 1997). In the late 1920s, after an earthquake leveled most of the city, the downtown was rebuilt according to a well-coordinated aesthetic plan that became the basis of strictly regulated development. The quality of life (largely expressed through issues of architecture, development, public amenities, and environment) has remained a public priority that has engaged the newspaper, the city council, and community organizations.

This communal sense was ruptured by the government leases for oil drilling off the coast and the almost-immediate oil spill in 1969 (Easton, 1972), which galvanized the community to activism. During this crisis three organizations were founded that remain cornerstones of Santa Barbara environmentalism: Get Oil Out (or GOO), which monitors and responds to threats arising from oil development and pollution; the Environmental Defense Fund (EDF), which monitors and responds to other environmental threats and land development throughout the region; and the Community Environmental Council (CEC), which engages in positive community development activities, such as recycling, hazardous waste collection, demonstration organic gardens, land use studies, and most recently a community indicators project.

These groups have provided state and national leadership in the environmental movement. They were, for example, early and significant players in the creation of Earth Day and in initiating recycling. The people who were active in the events of 1969 remain active in the town, region, and nation. Further, although the University of California at Santa Barbara was not as fully engaged in the 1969 oil spill as it might have been, it soon established the first environmental studies program, which to this day offers a vibrant undergraduate major. In recent years UCSB has established a professional school of environmental science and management, which offers graduate degrees. Santa Barbara itself is also home to an important national environmental policy center and several other environmental groups, organizations, and foundations. I give these details to indicate how deeply environmentalism is now embedded in the community's activities, values, and way of life.

The Community Environmental Council's capital campaign

To examine the kinds of appeals that have worked for environmental causes in the region, I interviewed Roe Anne White, current development director at CEC, and Sally Walker, who was paid consultant on a major capital campaign for the CEC about five years ago and on the 1996 effort to raise funds to acquire the largest remaining undeveloped coastal property in the city for use as a park and preserve—the area locally known as the Wilcox property, although it is now officially the Douglas Family Preserve. As a volunteer and officer of the local chapter of the Audubon Society, Walker has raised more modest pay-as-you-go funds for that organization. She has also worked as a fundraiser for a number of regional human service and cultural organizations. White has previously worked with private schools and arts fundraising in Los Angeles.

Before the capital campaign of 1991, CEC did not attempt systematic fundraising and development. From its inception, it had successfully supported itself largely on major grants and contracts from the government and private foundations, in recent years producing a half a million dollars a year. It also raised around $20,000 a year from annual membership fees of $20 to $25 and had an annual major gift of $50,000. But in 1991 CEC's board determined that approximately $750,000 was needed to pay off the mortgage for the organization's center, make repairs and improvements, equip a downtown recycling center, and expand some programs. Sally Walker began to professionalize fundraising at the organization and oversaw that goal's accomplishment in two and a half years.

One of Walker's first tasks was to help CEC's staff understand that fundraising was an "institutionwide commitment" to a public relations mindset. "The program staff needed to come to think of their work in terms of projects that could then be communicated to a potential funder," Walker says. To identify givers, she also needed to organize the records and establish a database that would track donor histories, keep track of and provide reminders for renewals and pledges, monitor cash flow and goal achievements, and provide names for future appeals (the cleaning up and development of the mailing list remains a continuing task). She beefed up membership benefits and designed fundraising literature for the capital campaign that had a distinctive look, different from earlier appeals from the organization. Finally, she also needed to develop volunteers because "all capital campaigns are volunteer-intensive."

Now I will focus on volunteers and the roles they served, because this issue seems to contain several interesting implications for the social relations involved in gift giving. Sally Walker particularly was concerned to "increase involvement from very prominent and qualified individuals." These qualified individuals served on committees that drew on their particular talents and professional networks and established a strong alliance between CEC fundraising and aspects of the volunteers' lives. Most impressive was the site development committee, including such people as a painting contractor, a developer, a landscape architect, and an owner of a home improvement center. They took charge of renovations, got bids, selected contractors, and oversaw some aspects of the work. In short, they provided highly professional contributions of specialized "expertise that no one on the staff or board had," said Walker. Further, by using their own professional connections they negotiated discounts and in-kind contributions, including ecologically appropriate technology such as outdoor lighting powered by solar panels. The members of this committee were enacting their own personal and professional commitments to environmentally sound construction and were able to enter into collaborations with suppliers who were interested in supporting green development and green construction trades.

Similarly, the "Burn the Mortgage" effort, essentially a major gifts committee, was headed by a vice president of a major investment brokerage. Because of his professional experience he was very comfortable in talking to people about money and giving. He was also able to enact his commitment to the town and the environment through his professional identity and skills.

One of the significant changes that occurred at this time was that the board, which had previously thought of itself as a group of activists, began to think of itself as potential givers and fundraisers. A couple of board members speaking to others then on the board—about a dozen people in all—were able to raise over $70,000 among themselves. Similar amounts were raised from prior board members.

Regularizing fundraising at the Community Environmental Council

Roe Anne White became permanent development director after the capital campaign met its goals in 1994. She continues to work with the board to build their fundraising potential through personal contacts, people to whom they might send relevant news articles with personal notes and whom they might invite to CEC receptions and lectures. The most promising contacts are invited to lunch at the headquarters with the director.

These initiatives illustrate what White characterizes as a standard principle of fundraising: "People give to people; they don't give to organizations." Information about the organization and its programs is provided in a series of brochures, newsletters, and pamphlets, which are distributed regularly and are available on a rack in the entryway to the center. These serve to provide supplementary information and keep donors aware of the organization's activities. Other materials are directly part of activities, such as a widely distributed pamphlet on nonpolluting means of pest control. As far as fundraising goes, however, the documents seem secondary to the personal contact. During the personal contact, White and the organization officers can speak directly to the interests and concerns of the gift-givers. About the values that drive environmental concern, she notes,

What I have found with the environment is that while many people are concerned with the environment, few open their pocketbooks to it as readily as one might expect. It is more challenging to raise money for an environmental organization than the other nonprofits I have worked for. For example, while the donor base is limited at an independent school, those involved are more likely to give because the gift directly benefits their children or grandchildren. It is clear that many Santa Barbarans care about the environment, but CEC's work, although addressing important environmental issues, does not have high visibility (like the Wilcox property or the current Oak issue).

Having a compelling need is a useful tool in fundraising. CEC has steadily addressed issues and problems for a quarter of a century, but it has had no urgent crisis to rally around since its founding after the oil spill in 1969. CEC also has a special fundraising challenge in that our work is so diverse. It ranges from community programs to research and technical assistance and is not explained with a few pat phrases. Additionally, although CEC has been in Santa Barbara for over twenty-eight years, it is a little-known organization. To enhance our fundraising effort, we need to articulate our mission more clearly, clarify the work CEC is doing, and get our name out into the community more effectively. Finally, with over five hundred nonprofits in Santa Barbara, there is a lot of competition for contributions in this community.

This is why building that sense of personal contact and ownership is important. Because most projects are carried out by staff there are only limited roles for volunteers, such as helping out with the gardens, doing office work, or getting involved in the art-from-scrap program. These volunteers are also not the same as the donors and are not likely to have the means for substantial contribution. Similarly, campaigns based on names gathered from various community events and programs have had low response rates. Nonetheless, a targeted appeal directed at twenty people who had been involved with CEC's garden program in the past did produce a 37 percent response rate, suggesting that commitments established earlier through activism and volunteerism may be reinvigorated and mobilized in other forms of commitment as people's life situations change. Part of the continuing analysis of the membership database is to locate those who have had continuing commitment through regular modest giving and may be now in a position to become major givers. Through such efforts the CEC now receives around $200,000 annually in donations and has a target of twice that.

To strengthen the sense of identity and ownership on the part of givers, four large "donor walls" at CEC's headquarters recognize major donors. In the library meeting room, one plaque identifies large givers to CEC's annual fund in the current year, distributed in four categories named after offshore islands. Another plaque identifies members of the Selma Rubin Society, named after a long-committed activist and founding board member who was the first to write the organization into her will. Members of this society have made planned gifts. These people are invited for an annual luncheon and receive letters from the director periodically to keep them updated and involved. This campaign is aimed at building endowment, which had been only $300 and now is approaching $100,000 in cash with $665,000 in anticipated gifts.

The first of two plaques in the office hallway identifies the major givers in the 1991 capital campaign in five categories ranging from benefactor to friend. The other lists about twenty corporate gift-givers to the newly established Corporate Council in four categories from corporate patron to corporate fellows. Major corporate givers include local banks and newspapers as well as refuse and recycling companies, landscape and architectural organizations, hotels, and businesses in other industries with a direct interest in environment and town quality of life. A number of companies have chosen to locate in town because of the quality of life, and some have become members of the Corporate Council. Roe Anne White explains, "From our earliest days, one of CEC's roles has been to ensure that the quality of life we enjoy in Santa Barbara is sustained. I initiated CEC's Corporate Council last year so that we could provide a forum for the business and environmental communities to come together to discuss issues important to both groups, while at the same time providing support for CEC's community programs."

The founding of the Corporate Council dovetails with a new major initiative being led by CEC in collaboration with a variety of individuals representing a number of interests. The Santa Barbara South Coast Community Indicators Project is modeled on similar programs in other communities designed to assess the overall health of the community. The project publishes a periodic volume and has a Web site that together create a portrait of the quality of life in the region based on existing social, economic, and environmental statistics. It provides a mechanism for various groups to monitor developments and engage in informed policy discussion both on particular issues and in a more holistic way. In creating this community portrait with the environment as a major component, CEC keeps environmental issues always on the policy table when any issue of community well-being arises and also makes clear to other community stakeholders their interest in maintaining and improving the environment.

Another new project, monitoring pollution in the watershed, also has potential impact on engaging targeted groups of people. The fundraising consequences of the watershed project are unclear because it is in its earliest development; however, it has already elicited one major gift from a regular CEC funder.

The Wilcox property campaign

The most spectacular fundraising effort in the region in recent years has been to raise the money for the acquisition of the Wilcox property. The effort suggests how much community identity and way of life are linked with environment and nature preservation and how extraordinary the gift giving can be if these associations are tapped so that people see giving as investing in their community.

A sixty-five-acre undeveloped property sitting on bluffs above a beach that is popular with local residents—though not frequented as much by tourists—had long been of concern to the adjoining suburban neighborhood. For a number of years it had been used as a nursery, but more recently it had been left fallow and open to community use for walking, dog running, ocean gazing, hang gliding, and other passive recreation. At least twice in the late 1980s bonds to purchase the land for a park failed the needed two-thirds majority by narrow margins. A number of plans for development had not been approved by the city and a lawsuit was filed by the owners, whose investment was being eaten up by the debt and the inability to use their property. In 1994, the county set aside $1 million of

Coastal Resource Enhancement Funds (originally oil mitigation funds obtained in a settlement with the oil companies) as seed money for direct purchase of the land if a local group led by the Small Wilderness Area Preserve (SWAP) could obtain matching funds. It was thought that the ultimate purchase price would be in excess of $5 million, and perhaps between $7 and $10 million.

After a year of almost no additional funds being raised, the city council was talking of reallocating some of the funds for another land purchase (*Santa Barbara News-Press,* 1995–1996). At this point, developers, perhaps suspecting that the preservationists were vulnerable, announced that they intended to develop the land as a single mansion. However, on January 18, 1996, the Trust for Public Land was able to arrange a last-ditch option to purchase the land at a low price of $3.5 million under the condition that the money be raised in six weeks—by February 29. Given the amount, the history, and the short deadline, this offer seemed almost certain to be an empty but politically useful gesture to clear the way for development.

SWAP and the trust needed to raise $2.5 million in six weeks. The state Department of Parks and Recreation immediately offered a $282,000 grant. Other state grants were sought but remained pending. Local politicians endorsed the effort. In the first four weeks over $370,000 was raised in private donations, for the most part in smaller gifts but also including one $100,000 donation. Much of it was collected at tables in front of local markets.

However, on February 14, with about two weeks remaining, an anonymous half-million-dollar gift gave the campaign an enormous boost and donations increased. As the deadline approached they were $600,000 short, which was made up by a single gift from Michael Douglas, the prominent actor, who lives in the area.

Sally Walker described the extraordinary nature of the campaign:

The Wilcox property . . . transformed the community. To this day, people will talk about the Wilcox campaign. And it evoked such synergy and such unselfish participation and sharing so broadly among the community. There was such a spontaneity to it that I don't think our community has ever seen anything like that . . . I've lived here twenty-one years and I've never [seen such] a mobilization of this community around an issue, and in such a positive, wholehearted sense. You are talking about in one and a half months going from about eight volunteers to about three thousand volunteers, going from virtually no donations to $3 million in donations, and it just swept the community with such passion and fervor that was unprecedented in my professional career, unprecedented in the history of any of the organizations involved in making this happen.

Why was this? What made it happen? I think it was a combination of things. Consistent public information. . . . The media carried this constantly. This was a great service. They followed it so doggedly and so prominently. And people were writing letters to the editor daily. There were articles almost every day on the editorial page, in Barney Brantingham's column [Brantingham is a local columnist who has become a kind of insider's voice about town life], on the editorial page, and the front of the second section. TV stations were constantly after us for updated information.

An examination of the *Santa Barbara News-Press* (1995–1996) confirms the strong media support. Front-page articles appearing weekly during the early part of the campaign turned into almost every other day occurrences during the final two weeks, and they were accompanied by editorials and letters to the editor. Moreover, the stories regularly included a sidebar—a shaded box providing information on how to cooperate. Many of these stories seemed orchestrated to create excitement about the property and campaign—describing the beauty and value of the property, the community concern over the years, and the excitement generated by the campaign. Barney Brantingham not only devoted a number of columns to supporting the campaign but was also directly in contact with SWAP. The newspaper was deeply involved in "boosterism" on this issue, presenting the property and the campaign as matters of civic importance, pride, and part of Santa Barbara's way of life.

Similarly, the January 25, 1996, issue of the community events weekly, the *Santa Barbara Independent*, announced the possibility of the land purchase and the campaign to raise funds in a long cover-page feature story on "The Twenty Greatest Environmental Hits of Santa Barbara," clearly setting the stage for a new mobilization in the tradition of the city rebuilding in the 1920s and the response to the oil spill in 1969. The local TV news also carried the story regularly, and the cable company posted frequent announcements on the community bulletin board that accompanies its programming schedule scroll.

This kind of excitement supported by the media carried through in the community in neighborhood meetings run by SWAP, leafleting campaigns, individually arranged fundraising dinners in homes and in restaurants, apple juice sales at the entrance of the property (children sold the juice for $5 a glass), and pledge tables at the organic markets, specialty foods stores, and the supermarkets. Small gifts generated by such activities provided somewhere in the range of $1 million. Many of these smaller gifts actually reflected individuals "giving at their highest potential. People who really cared about this. We had a lot of small gifts but also a lot of gifts of $1,000 or more. This really captured the public imagination," says Walker.

Over $1.1 million was provided by two major gifts, and several local foundations provided several other substantial grants. To seek this money, Sally Walker used a small edition showbook prepared by the Trust for Public Land. About thirty copies were made of this twelve-page collection of photographs, maps, and letters of support. The book displayed the natural beauty of the land and its importance to the community life. Walker comments, "We needed to show the beauty of this place to seek gifts from people who had never walked the property. It helped that it was on TV. . . . Photographs of the serenity and the beauty of this property were very important for Michael Douglas's gift and the other major anonymous gift."

Also very important to the major givers was the excitement and support expressed to that point through community fundraising. Walker says, "The reason that these two $600,000 dollar gifts came was because it was clear to everyone that there was so much will in the community to make this happen."

When asked to characterize the motivations of two major givers, Walker commented, "Very quickly this project came to mean more than just a piece of land, it came to mean. . . . it became a community identity issue. It was a 'my God, what does this community stand for.' It came to embody community spirit. It came to embody a lot of things for people. It came to embody empowerment—about people feeling empowered to dramatically do something on their watch. . . . It was just waking up to this realization that all the great environmental victories in our community were won in the past by people on their watch, and what were we going to do on our watch." And in describing the meaning of this campaign to the larger community she said,

What kind of community do we want to be—that is really what you want people to think about when you are doing environmental fundraising. . . . Who are we? What do we care about? What is important here? And that as individuals we have the ability to make a tremendous difference. And the Wilcox property made that clear. We have the ability to make a difference. That feeling and tone was carried and it sustained this project in a way that no one before had really seen. Maybe back in the past when some of the big environmental issues had come, but this involved a lot of fundraising. It didn't involve lobbying a city body or a county body and winning it by going to city council and county board of supervisors meetings. This was won in the hearts and minds and homes and wallets of the city residents.

Conclusions

The Wilcox property campaign provides a striking example of how individuals and a community can be moved to extraordinary giving when the issue becomes one of maintaining and advancing a communal way of life: building on individual and community values and the psychic rewards for doing good, but moving beyond that to investing in the kind of community one wants to live in and the lifestyle one wants to share. Helping to create this kind of meaning for the campaign was the long history of community acts to protect the environment, create a way of life that recognizes the environment as a key element, and establish a tradition of action and commitment. This meaning was also fostered by the support of the forums of community life (newspapers, television, city government, politicians), which saw themselves as part of the community and potentially strong agents in continuing the tradition of action. Individuals and activist groups carried through these meanings, traditions, and opportunities to engage wide public participation and to tap the resources of individuals in a position to make major gifts. All these forces worked together to create and mutually support a set of meanings that extended beyond the boundaries of normal gift giving.

There are elements of this kind of association between gift giving and way of life in the more usual fundraising efforts of the Community Environmental Council. In a few instances, CEC was able to draw on the participants' engagement with a way of life: when the board of directors was transformed from a group of community activists into a group that also was a source of giving and the center of a network of potential givers; when people who had earlier been garden volunteers gave gifts in order to allow their early work to continue; and when people in the building and architectural trades who were committed to environmentally sound development of those industries gave of their expertise, clout, and money in an energized and committed way. CEC's Corporate Council and the Community Indicators Project hold great promise for building an even stronger connection between community life and environmental causes.

Yet the CEC example also suggests that activism and engagement with a way of life does not always lead to financial support. Volunteers and activists who gave their time and attention did not necessarily give money. Only if they were engaged in activities that drew together their value commitments with the concept of investment in community life did substantial giving result. The emotional satisfactions of doing good and healing ruptures can be experienced as private acts of virtue, quite independent from one's community. Similarly, one's way of life can be seen primarily as a matter of individual choices and individual means. But when the way of life is seen as the consequence of community endeavors and, therefore, as a community responsibility, individuals can come to see that personal investment in a way of life means investing in communal projects.

Positive words about communal investment in communal life cannot in themselves create a communal culture and real projects that build the communal life—particularly in a society so deeply committed to individual action, individual values, and individual advancement. But if we are aware of the great potential of unfolding events to draw people to have a personal stake in communal action, we can develop a rhetoric that makes the value of communal investment stronger and more visible. And the people who buy into the communal investment can receive very powerful psychic rewards indeed.

References

Bazerman, C. "Some Informal Comments on Texts Mediating Fundraising Relationships: Cultural Sites of Affiliation." Working papers. Indianapolis: Indiana Center on Philanthropy, 1997.

Easton, R. *Black Tide: The Santa Barbara Oil Spill and Its Consequences.* New York: Delacorte Press, 1972.

Kelly, K. "From Motivation to Mutual Understanding." In D. Burlingame (ed.), *Critical Issues in Fundraising.* New York: Wiley, 1997.

Molotch, H., Freudenburg, W., and Paulsen, K. "History Repeats Itself, but How? City Character, Urban Tradition, and the Accomplishment of Place." Unpublished manuscript, University of California, Santa Barbara, 1997.

Santa Barbara News-Press, Dec. 1, 1995–Mar. 11, 1996.

"The Twenty Greatest Environmental Hits of Santa Barbara." *Santa Barbara Independent,* Jan. 25, 1996, pp. 3ff.

CHARLES BAZERMAN, *professor of English and education at the University of California, Santa Barbara, specializes in rhetoric and social theory, the rhetoric of science and technology, and teaching writing.*

A content analysis of the arguments used in fundraising letters reveals how fundraisers resolve the altruism versus exchange models of persuasion, the organizational patterns of their arguments, and the degree to which they use emotional and logical proofs.

2

Content analysis of fundraising letters

Donald N. Ritzenhein

THE DIRECT MAIL LETTER is a staple of fundraising for almost any nonprofit organization. Such letters are the most common way to ask middle-class people to donate money (Flanagan, 1993).

Perhaps because of the extensive use of direct mail letters, there are many experts in philanthropy who give advice on how to use language in fundraising letters to "entice" donors to "respond with a check" (Cone, 1987, p. 1). Clark (1993), for example, advises fundraisers on such matters as copy length, readability, voice, attention getting, emotion, belonging, and credibility as elements in direct mail solicitation. Cover (1980) urges fundraisers to appeal to the special interests of alumni. Schneiter (1985) advises fundraisers to write letters that talk about benefits—how donors will have the satisfaction of knowing their gifts are being used for good purposes.

For the practitioner, there are limitations to this easily available advice. A lot of it tends to be anecdotal, based largely on someone's experience as a fundraiser and his or her best sense of what "works"

NEW DIRECTIONS FOR PHILANTHROPIC FUNDRAISING, NO. 22, WINTER 1998 © JOSSEY-BASS PUBLISHERS

and does not work. Smith and Cockriel (1987) conclude that most research into fundraising, at least in higher education, is of this highly personal nature and does not improve our knowledge to the level that more formal research would.

To address these limitations, I conducted a study to find out, in a systematic way, what my fundraising colleagues are actually writing in their direct mail letters. Specifically, the study reported here addressed four research questions: What kinds of arguments do fundraisers use, and with what frequency do they use them, in their direct mail letters? Into what organizational pattern, if any, are these arguments placed? What is the mix of emotion and logical proof used to support these arguments, and what specific kinds of support are used for each type of proof? To what extent do fundraisers base their arguments on rewards to donors in exchange for their gifts?

I did not seek to test any hypothesis because there is so little previous research and no real basis for making theoretical predictions about how fundraisers deal with rhetorical issues.

Methodology

Content analysis is the methodology that was used in this study. Content analysis is a research technique for drawing conclusions from data that are both replicable (reliable) and valid. The technique involves breaking down texts into smaller sampling units based on a definition of what constitutes a unit, developing a set of categories to which each unit can be assigned, selecting and training independent coders who examine each unit and assign it to its appropriate category, testing the reliability of the coders' decisions, and then analyzing and drawing conclusions from the resulting category assignments (see Krippendorff, 1980).

There have been numerous content-analytic studies of various kinds of direct mail appeals, including political campaigns (Ringer, 1986; Cutbirth and Rasmussen, 1982; Schmidt and Schmidt, 1983), the Equal Rights Amendment (Smith, 1982), and magazine query letters (Jolliffe, 1992), among others. No content-analytic studies of direct mail fundraising, however, were found. Ramsberger (1987) conducted an experimental study to evaluate the effectiveness of moral (altruistic), nonmoral (exchange), and social motivations for a health cause. He was trying to determine donor responses, however, and not what fundraisers actually practice.

A related methodology, but one that should not be confused with content analysis, is *discourse analysis*. There are several discourse-analytic studies of fundraising appeals in this volume, and the authors have defined the methodology in their studies. At least one other discourse-analytic study worth noting is by Buchanan (1995). His examination of the discourse of fundraising, including the discourse of asking, leads him to conclude that there has been a shift away from obligation models to exchange models among fundraisers. The limitation of his study—which is also a limitation of discourse studies in general—is the small amount of data on which he bases his conclusions and the rather personal nature of the analysis he uses to examine the data. Discourse analyses are provocative introductions to possible areas of inquiry, but because they are essentially case studies generalizations are probably best limited to the scope of data they examine.

For this study, twenty-one direct mail fundraising letters published in Torre and Bendixen's *Direct Mail Fundraising: Letters That Work* (1988) were used. They were evenly divided among hospitals, universities, and community service agencies. The unit of analysis within each letter was an argument, defined as a complete unit of proof including data, a reasoning process, and a conclusion (Ziegelmueller, Kay, and Dause, 1990). I identified 190 arguments for coding. Three coders examined each of the 190 arguments according to instructions I provided them. Coders evaluated each argument using four categories.

The first coding category was the kind of reason offered by each argument. An examination of the letters revealed that thirteen distinct reasons were used. Coders were asked to identify which of these reasons best described each argument. The reason categories were quality of the institution; needs of the institution; urgency, the need to give now; matching gifts are possible if you give; your gift matters, it will make a difference; incentives to give (taxes, honors, and so on); you have an obligation to give; give because others have already given; we use gift money wisely; give in honor of someone; giving is in your self-interest; the "ask" itself; a thank-you for past or future gifts.

The second category of analysis was the type of data, or proof, used in each argument. Coders were asked to identify which of eight types of proof were used in each argument: statistics; real example; hypothetical example; testimony; statement of fact; reference to a brochure; other (not defined by coders); no proof offered.

The third category was the basis of proof, whether emotional or logical. The final category was the motivation behind each argument—that is, whether an argument suggested that the donor would receive some kind of reward for giving.

Intercoder reliability was calculated for each of the four categories of analysis using Corsi's R. Initial reliability for the first category, reasons, was 65.4 percent; reliability improved to 80.2 percent when the thirty-five unusable arguments were excluded. Initial reliability for the second category, proof, was 73.1 percent, which improved to 82.2 percent when the twenty-two unusable arguments were excluded. Reliability for the basis of proof was 85.4 percent, and 86.6 percent for the motivation category. Overall initial reliability was 77.6 percent, which improved to 83.6 percent for the arguments actually used for analysis.

Research findings

The first research question was, "What kinds of arguments are used to persuade prospects to give?" Overall, the thirteen choices offered in the reason category scheme represented the scope of arguments used in the direct mail solicitations sampled for this study. Of course, further coding of additional letters may reveal other arguments that did not surface in these letters.

The more important question, however, is the frequency of arguments, by type, that are used by fundraisers. The following list displays frequency distribution of arguments, by reasons given:

Quality of institution	22 percent
Your gift matters	19 percent
Needs we address	18 percent
Ask and thank you	15 percent
Incentive for giving	7 percent
Giving is in donor's self-interest	5 percent
Your gift will be matched	4 percent
You have an obligation to give	3 percent
Join others	3 percent
There is an urgency, we need your gift now	2 percent
Testimony of others	2 percent
We are accountable	2 percent

Of the thirteen types of argument, four constituted 70 percent of the arguments used: arguments that emphasize the quality of the institution, arguments that suggest the donor's gift matters and will allow the organization to reach its goals, arguments that focus on the needs of the organization, and the argument that simply asks for a gift. The remaining nine arguments together accounted for 30 percent of the total arguments used.

The importance of the "quality" and "need" arguments was further evidenced by the fact that every one of the sample letters included one or both of these arguments. Moreover, 76 percent of the letters had at least one instance of the argument "your gift matters," and 66.6 percent of the letters used at least one direct "ask."

The next research question was whether there was a pattern of arguments used by fundraisers in their direct mail letters. The authors began their letters with either a quality or need argument 71 percent of the time, and they ended 57 percent of their letters with an ask. In letters where the "your gift matters" argument appeared, the argument was in the middle of the letters 62.5 percent of the time. Five patterns accounted for 71 percent of the letters: quality-need-gift matters (24 percent); quality-gift matters-ask (19 percent); quality-need-gift matters-ask (9.5 percent); quality-ask (9.5 percent); need-quality-gift matters (9.5 percent).

The third research question was whether fundraisers used emotional or logical forms of proof, and if both, in what proportion. Just under 60 percent of the arguments relied on emotional proof (59.5 percent); the balance relied on logical proof. Of course, judgments of whether an argument is based on logic or emotion stem from the coders, and may not be what the authors intended. However, intercoder reliability was fairly high (85.4) and the 60–40 split has a certain face validity to it: it is the kind of result we might have expected in a persuasive message intended to move the reader to engage in a specific act, usually in immediate response to an appeal.

A second part of this question involved whether any specific kinds of support tended to be associated with emotional versus logical arguments. The percentage frequency of each of the six types of support, plus "none," for each of the two types of proof (emotional and logical) are shown in Table 2.1.

Sixty percent of emotional arguments were not supported with any type of supporting material, whereas nearly 75 percent of logical arguments were. When supporting material was used for emotional arguments, the proof tended to be in the form of examples and specific facts. Facts were also the dominant form of support for logical arguments, followed by statistics.

Table 2.1. Percentage of emotional and logical arguments supported by proof

	Emotional Argument	Logical Argument
Statistics	2.7 percent	13.6 percent
Examples	14.9 percent	6.1 percent
Testimony	5.4 percent	3.0 percent
Facts	14.9 percent	47.0 percent
Brochure	0.0 percent	4.5 percent
Other	1.4 percent	0.0 percent
None	60.8 percent	25.8 percent
Total	100.0 percent	100.0 percent

The final research question was to what extent arguments were based on reward-motivation, defined to include such things as recognition, tax deductions, and quid pro quo items. Only 13.4 percent of the arguments used in the sample letters offered rewards to donors in exchange for their gifts.

Discussion and implications

Kenneth Burke (1945) provides a rhetorical theory that may help us understand the findings reported here. Burke's theory of rhetoric stems from his belief that we use language as a strategic response to a situation (Brock, 1990). When fundraisers create direct mail letters, they are selecting language as a strategic response to the situation of having to raise funds on behalf of the institutions they serve.

One of the primary tools Burke has provided rhetoricians as a way of understanding the strategic use of language is the *Dramatistic Pentad:* act, scene, agent, agency, and purpose. The Dramatistic Pentad is a way of addressing five core questions when one wants to persuade someone to engage in any human action:

- What is it that is to be done? (the act)
- When or where is it to be done? (the scene)
- Who is to do it? (the agent)
- How is it do be done? (agency)
- Why is it to be done? (purpose)

The following statement, using the Pentad, summarizes the basic appeal of fundraising letters based on the content analysis presented in the previous section: *Given social needs* (scene) *or an organization of high quality* (scene), *a prospective donor* (agent) *is asked to contribute* (act) *money* (agency) *so the organization can address those needs or maintain its high quality* (purpose).

According to Burke, if we carefully study a persuasive message we will often find that the persuader focuses on one of the terms, or will pair two terms together, like scene-act or scene-agent, which Burke calls a *ratio*. The terms that are featured in a persuasive appeal can give us an insight into the philosophy of the person who is trying to persuade others. For example, in his classic study of Senator Edward Kennedy's 1969 Chappaquiddick speech, Ling (1980) describes how Senator Kennedy emphasized the scene, or situation (that is, the swift, dark river into which his car, along with Mary Jo Kopechne, had plunged), as one over which he had no control and in response to which he was a victim. In addition, Kennedy stressed that the agents, or voters of Massachusetts, rather than he, himself, were in control of his future.

Based on the findings of this study, it is clear that fundraisers try to persuade donors based on a scene-act ratio that "either calls for acts in keeping with scenes or scenes in keeping with acts" (Burke, 1945, p. 9). Recall that 71 percent of the letters began with descriptions of the scene, expressed either as the social needs the organization was trying to cure or the high quality of the institution itself. That description was followed by an appeal for the donor to act in response to the scene, that a gift was necessary in order for the organization to address its social needs or maintain or improve its high quality. Fundraisers apparently believe that if they describe their organization (scene) accurately and compellingly, their prospects will give, an act that is in keeping with the described scene.

Understanding that fundraisers use a scene-act ratio as the basis for motivating donors, we can also see what they do not use as the basis for motivating donors. For example, it has been suggested that the more promising theories of donor behavior involve exchange models as opposed to altruistic models (Brittingham and Pezzullo, 1990). Buchanan (1995), cited earlier, expresses concern over this shift. However, when viewed through the lens of the Pentad, the fundraisers whose letters were used in this study did not base their appeals primarily on either altruism or exchange models of motivation.

If altruism had been the dominant appeal in the fundraising letters, we would see arguments reflecting the Pentadic form of the agent-act ratio. When using the agent-act ratio, the persuader is focusing on a person's character and how that character requires the performance of the desired act (Foss, Foss, and Trapp, 1991). Some of the arguments were of this type. For example, note in these arguments the focus on agent, or character, of the person being asked to give a gift (Torre and Bendixen, 1988, reproduced with permission):

You are an outstanding example of the University's commitment to holistic education and to its Baptist heritage.

Because it's your prayerful financial support that keeps the Mission door open 365 days each year.

I hope you will give this some thought in the days ahead—that your response will reflect your values and commitment to SUNY Optometry.

In contrast, if the exchange model had been the dominant appeal in the fundraising letters used in this study, we would see arguments reflecting the Pentadic form of the agency-agent ratio. A focus on agency, how donors will be recognized or rewarded for their gift, is always central to the exchange, or quid pro quo, appeal. Recall that only 13.4 percent of the arguments used by fundraisers involved rewards for donors. We can see in those arguments the focus on agency, or means of recognition or reward. For example (from Torre and Bendixen, 1988; reproduced with permission):

I would like to add your name to our Honor Roll of Donors.

A gift of $500 or more will place your name, or the name you choose, on an attractive plaque in the entrance to the activities center.

And when you send your gift we will send you an informative brochure, called "Here's to Your Health." It lists seven steps you can take to enjoy better health and a longer life.

Although arguments focusing on the agent-act (altruistic) and the agency-agent (exchange) motives were used, they were not the primary pattern of argument. Rather than choose between these two opposite means of persuasion, the rhetorical choice of fundraisers, based on the data in this study, is to rely on the scene-act ratio, which ignores issues of altruism or exchange and calls for action rooted in the scene (situation) of need or quality.

The second research question was what pattern of arguments was used. What emerges from the patterns of argument described here, which are variations on a quality-need-matters-ask sequence, is that fundraisers, either consciously or not, are using Monroe's Motivated Sequence (Monroe and Ehninger, 1967) as their basic organizational scheme. Where Burke was a philosopher, Monroe was a psychologist, and his rhetorical sequence is influenced by his observations about how, psychologically, we go about solving problems that face us.

The Motivated Sequence begins with an attention step, strategies that focus our interest on the speaker's or writer's topic. Fundraising letters begin with an attention step that references the institution's existing high quality or the need for help. The next step in the sequence is the need step. In by far the majority of their letters, fundraisers focus on the needs of their organization. Monroe's satisfaction step is fulfilled with arguments about how giving to the institution will allow it to meet its needs. Monroe's visualization step is fulfilled with the "your gift matters" argument used in a majority of the letters. Finally, Monroe proposes an action step, which is met when fundraisers ask prospects for a gift.

Not every letter in this study followed this pattern exactly. However, there is sufficient overall consistency of the "quality-need-your gift matters-ask" pattern to justify the conclusion that direct mail letters generally use a Motivated Sequence pattern. Knowing this natural tendency, fundraisers may be able to evaluate their work more carefully against the criteria of the Motivated Sequence to be sure they have maximized its potential for arranging their arguments.

Third, what do we make of the 60–40 split between emotional and logical proofs? If we substitute the term *activation* for emotional proof and *cognition* for logical proof, as Cronkhite (1968) suggests, we see that fundraisers believe their prospects require a high level of activation—but not without some logical basis for understanding what they are being asked to do. It appears that fundraisers avoid both extremes—of naively assuming their prospects only need logical reasons to act and of assuming their prospects are motivated solely by emotional appeals.

Fundraisers do not generally support their emotional appeals with examples, testimony, or other forms of supporting material. This is not surprising. Sources of activation stem from such things as beliefs and attitudes ("our strong Baptist heritage" in one letter), language style ("these kids win . . . their families and friends win . . . we all win"), and expressions of appreciation ("thank you for your interest in helping to shape the lives of our precious children"), among others.

Finally, this study examined the frequency of arguments rooted in reward appeals. Based on a content analysis of a collection of letters, reward-based appeals are used some of the time but are by no means the dominant form of persuasion.

Summary and conclusions

Kelly (1991) has criticized contemporary studies of philanthropy for their obsession with the attitudes and motivations of donors, and what she considers a fruitless search for the "magic bullet" of fundraising success (p. 115). This study is a departure from such traditional attitude-and-motivation research because it asks the question, "What do fundraisers think persuades donors and how do they try to accomplish that task?" As Rubin, Rubin, and Piele (1990) suggest, content analysis may not tell us much about the effects of a message, but it can tell us a lot about those who create the message.

Although this study did not begin with hypotheses about what fundraisers think persuades donors, it generated the following conclusions, which can be used as hypotheses for further studies:

• Fundraisers base their appeals on Burke's scene-act ratio, wherein an act (giving) is expected to follow from a clear and compelling description of a scene (situation).
• By using a scene-act ratio, fundraisers reject both altruistic (agent-act) and exchange (agency-agent) models of persuasion.

- Fundraisers arrange their arguments according to the Monroe Motivated Sequence.
- Fundraisers use emotional arguments more than logical ones (60–40), but rely on both.
- Rewards for giving are offered by fundraisers, but only as sub-text to the main force of argument, which is rooted in the needs of the organization or its high quality.

Future content-analytic studies should be done to test these hypotheses on an even broader collection of fundraising letters. In addition, it would be interesting to know whether different types of organizations use different Pentadic ratios. For example, one has a sense that public television and public radio rely more on exchange models (agency-agent) in their heavy use of premiums for giving, and that religious organizations rely more on altruistic (agent-act) appeals in their call for tithing or giving based on moral obligation. The other hypotheses generated by this study could also be tested with similar subsets of fundraising letters.

Studying arguments as this study did is an important part of understanding the rhetoric of fundraising appeals, but it is not the only element fundraisers pay attention to in their direct mail pieces. Content-analytic studies should be done on the language style used in letters as well as on visual and tactile elements employed by fundraisers.

References

Brittingham, B. E., and Pezzullo, T. R. *The Campus Green: Fundraising in Higher Education.* Washington, D.C.: George Washington University, School of Education and Human Development, 1990. (ASHE-ERIC Higher Education Report no. 1)

Brock, B. L. "Rhetorical Criticism: A Burkean Approach Revisited." In B. L. Brock, R. L. Scott, and J. W. Chesebro (eds.), *Methods of Rhetorical Criticism: A Twentieth-Century Perspective.* (3rd ed., rev.) Detroit: Wayne State University Press, 1990.

Buchanan, A. E. "The Language of Fundraising." In D. Elliott (ed.), *The Ethics of Asking.* Baltimore, Md.: Johns Hopkins University Press, 1995.

Burke, K. *A Grammar of Motives.* Englewood Cliffs, N.J.: Prentice Hall, 1945.

Clark, C. "How to Prepare a Direct Mail Solicitation." In M. J. Worth (ed.), *Educational Fundraising: Principles and Practices.* Phoenix: Oryx Press, 1993.

Cone, A. L. Jr. *How to Create and Use Solid Gold Fund-Raising Letters.* Ambler, Pa.: Fund-Raising Institute, 1987.

Cover, N. Jr. "Direct Mail: Growing Up in a Time of Crisis." In P. A. Welch (ed.), *Increasing Annual Giving.* San Francisco: Jossey-Bass, 1980.

Cronkhite, G. L. "Logic, Emotion, and the Paradigm of Persuasion." In J. M. Anderson and P. J. Dovre (eds.), *Readings in Argumentation.* Needham Heights, Mass.: Allyn & Bacon, 1968.

Cutbirth, C. W., and Rasmussen, C. "Political Direct Mail: The State of the Art." Paper presented at the annual meeting of the Central States Speech Association, Milwaukee, 1982. (ED 217 498)

Flanagan, J. *Successful Fundraising: A Complete Handbook for Volunteers and Professionals.* Chicago: Contemporary Books, 1993.

Foss, S. K., Foss, K. A., and Trapp, R. *Contemporary Perspectives on Rhetoric.* (2nd ed.) Prospect Heights, Ill.: Waveland Press, 1991.

Jolliffe, L. "Persuasive Elements of One Hundred Successful Magazine Query Letters." Paper presented at the annual meeting of the Association for Education in Journalism and Mass Communication, Montreal, Quebec, Canada, Aug. 1992. (ED 351 676)

Kelly, K. *Fundraising and Public Relations: A Critical Analysis.* Hillsdale, N.J.: Erlbaum, 1991.

Krippendorff, K. *Content Analysis: An Introduction to Its Methodology.* Thousand Oaks, Calif.: Sage, 1980.

Ling, D. A. "A Pentadic Analysis of Senator Edward Kennedy's Address to the People of Massachusetts, July 25, 1969." In B. L. Brock and R. L. Scott (eds.), *Methods of Rhetorical Criticism: A Twentieth-Century Perspective.* (2nd ed., rev.) Detroit: Wayne State University Press, 1980.

Monroe, A. H., and Ehninger, D. *Principles and Types of Speech.* (6th ed.) Glenview, Ill.: Scott, Foresman, 1967.

Ramsberger, P. F. "The Social Psychology of Direct Mail Fundraising." Unpublished doctoral dissertation, George Washington University, 1987.

Ringer, R. J. "The Language of Fund-Raising Direct Mail: Differences Between Letters for National and Local Constituencies." Paper presented at the annual meeting of the International Communication Association, Chicago, May 1986. (ED 291 117)

Rubin, R. B., Rubin, A. M., and Piele, L. J. *Communication Research: Strategies and Sources.* (2nd ed.) Belmont, Calif.: Wadsworth, 1990.

Schmidt, M. S., and Schmidt, M. J. "Applications of Direct Mail in Voter Turnout Activities." Paper presented at the annual meeting of the International Communication Association, Dallas, May 1983. (ED 233 402)

Schneiter, P. H. *The Art of Asking: How to Solicit Philanthropic Gifts.* (2nd ed.) Ambler, Pa.: Fund-Raising Institute, 1985.

Smith, C. M., and Cockriel, I. W. "A Content Analysis of Fundraising Manuscripts in Higher Education." Unpublished report, 1987. (ED 290 404)

Smith, L. "NOW vs. Stop ERA: Unequal Messages on the Equal Rights Amendment, January–June 1982." Paper presented at the annual meeting of the Association of Education in Journalism and Mass Communication, Gainesville, Fla., Aug. 1982. (ED 246 434)

Torre, R. L., and Bendixen, M. A. *Direct Mail Fundraising: Letters That Work.* New York: Plenum, 1988.

Ziegelmueller, G., Kay, J. and Dause, C. *Argumentation: Inquiry and Advocacy.* (2nd ed.) Englewood Cliffs, N.J.: Prentice Hall, 1990.

DONALD N. RITZENHEIN *is interim vice president for development and alumni affairs at Wayne State University in Detroit, Michigan.*

The careful use of metaphors is not new to fundrais-
ing discourse. This chapter shows the function and
assumptions underlying common metaphors in
fundraising discourse.

3

Conceptual metaphor and the discourse of philanthropy

Peter McCagg

What one finds in language depends in large measure
on what one expects to find.
—Ronald W. Langacker, *Foundations of Cognitive*
Grammar

WHAT I EXPECT TO FIND in the discourse of philanthropy is shaped
by the lenses of cognitive linguistics, experiential realism, and most
specifically, conceptual metaphor. Cognitive linguistics takes the
ability to recognize similarities and the ability to form categories
as basic to human cognition. Experiential realism considers meaning to be embodied—that is, it takes the view that categories do not
exist independent of the observer-experiencer but are in large part
a consequence of our having the sorts of bodies and perceptual
capabilities that we are endowed with as human beings. Technically,
it is argued by cognitive linguists that the categories formed by the
human mind are structured in terms of *image schemas* (for example,
abstract paths and containers, and notions such as centrality and
marginality and balance), the predicate-argument structures of

NEW DIRECTIONS FOR PHILANTHROPIC FUNDRAISING, NO. 22, WINTER 1998 © JOSSEY-BASS PUBLISHERS

propositions (entities related to one another via the semantics of abstract predicates), *metonymies* (use of one salient aspect of an experience to stand for or refer to other aspects of that experience), and *metaphors*. It is this last aspect of human categorization, conceptual metaphor, that I wish to use as a way into examining the discourse of a small sample of philanthropic texts—letters and other promotional materials for not-for-profit organizations—presented for the consideration of a group of rhetoricians and linguists who gathered at Indiana University–Purdue University Indianapolis in the fall of 1997.

In cognitive linguistics, metaphors are understood as conventional (that is, subconscious and automatically processed) correspondences across conceptual domains in which generally more abstract concepts are understood through generally more concretely structured concepts—understanding "justice," for example, partially in terms of "balance." (See Lakoff and Johnson, 1980; Lakoff, 1987; and Lakoff and Turner, 1989, for elaboration of this definition.) It is important to emphasize that metaphor involves *partial* understanding of one *kind* of thing in terms of another *kind* of thing. The partial nature of metaphorical understanding, combined with its conventionality—that is, that we typically are unaware of how metaphor works in shaping our understanding of our experiences—are the primary sources of both the power and the potential danger of metaphor. Metaphor focuses our attention on only one aspect of some abstract experience, highlighting that aspect and at the same time downplaying or hiding other facets of it. It is this quality of metaphor that is manipulated by politicians and advertisers, for example, to seduce targeted audiences into seeing things in the particular light that the politician or advertiser wishes while at the same time making it less likely that the targeted audiences will notice other facets of the ideas or products presented. It is this quality of metaphor that those who would persuade others to part with their money for one cause or another might benefit from understanding better and incorporating more consciously into their public discourses. I hasten to add that this is not a call to deception; it is rather an attempt to heighten awareness among practitioners in the fundraising field about the ways that metaphor works and, ultimately, how metaphor can be used to further one's causes.

For much of Western history, metaphor has been looked upon with suspicion by philosophers as being a seductive device that prevents people from seeing things the way they "really" or "objectively" are. It has been argued within objectivist schools of philosophy that, in order to get better at the truth, metaphor should be eliminated from discourse altogether. The following quote by Samuel Parker illustrates this attitude: "All those Theories in Philosophy which are expressed only in metaphorical Termes are not real Truths, but the meer products of Imagination, dress'd up (like Christmas babies) in a few spangled empty words. . . . Thus their wanton and luxuriant fancies climbing up into the Bed of Reason, do not only defile it by unchaste and illegitimate Embraces, but instead of real conceptions and notices of Things, impregnate the mind with nothing but Ayerie and Subventaneous Phantasmes" (1666, quoted in Lakoff and Johnson, 1980, p. 191).

Readers may be struck by the irony arising from the preponderance of metaphor that has "climbed wantonly" up into Parker's own "bed of reason" in this warning about the danger of metaphor. His words, although not proof, offer some evidence of the impossibility of avoiding metaphors even in an attempt to discredit them.

Until recently, linguists, at best, have treated metaphor as a peripheral matter, not something central to the enterprise of understanding. In the view of metaphor put forth by Lakoff and Johnson in their widely read and cited book *Metaphors We Live By* (1980), both of these positions are challenged (that is, that metaphor is undesirable in rational discourse and that it is unimportant in the study of language). Lakoff and Johnson argue that metaphor is both central to the enterprise of linguistics and absolutely fundamental to all thinking that goes beyond expressing thoughts about our direct experiences of physical space and sensation. Lakoff (1993) states this view in fairly direct and strong terms: "Metaphor is the main mechanism through which we comprehend abstract concepts and perform abstract reasoning" (p. 244). Without attempting to verify this claim, I shall work from the assumption that a metaphorical account of the discourse of fundraising can provide insights for practitioners about how they do and how they might address their audiences.

Specifically, I shall sketch a rough Lakovian metaphorical analysis for the promotional documents of two nonprofit organizations, Habitat for Humanity and Purdue University's Black Cultural Center (BCC), and also for a sample of fundraising letters. I hope to be able to show what such an analysis reveals about how the producers of these texts conceptualize their subjects and their audiences. The materials examined were included in a packet of fundraising materials provided to participants at the 1997 working session referred to earlier.

Before looking at the language and metaphor found in these documents, however, I believe outlining two sorts of background information may be useful. The first of these is a consideration of the three types of conceptual metaphor defined by Lakoff and Johnson (1980): *orientational*, *ontological*, and *structural*. The second is presentation of a framework for understanding morality in metaphorical terms based on the work of Mark Johnson in *Moral Imagination* (1993) and that of Lakoff in *Moral Politics* (1996).

Orientational metaphor

Orientational metaphors are metaphors that organize a whole system of concepts in terms of physical, bodily experienced spatial relations. In fact, orientational metaphors are among the best examples of how metaphorical concepts are "embodied." Our conceptualization of "well-being" is one case that would appear to have particular relevance for philanthropic discourse. We can (and most commonly do) understand happiness, for example, as well as health, having control over ourselves and others, quantity and goodness all in terms of vertical space (that is, UP-DOWN orientation). Evidence for the existence of these metaphors may be seen in the following examples:

Happy is up/sad is down:
My spirits rose/fell when I heard the good/bad news.
I am feeling up/down today.

Health is up/sickness is down:
I'm in tip-top condition.
I've come down with the flu.

Control is up/lack of control is down:
He gained control over his emotions.
His anger gained the upper hand.

More is up/less is down:
Prices are rising/falling.
We are fundraising.

Good is up/bad is down:
This is high/low quality work.

Orientational metaphors are so basic to the way we understand things that we usually do not even recognize the sort of language represented in these examples as being metaphorical at all. A moment's reflection, however, ought to allow one to see that what I suspect is one of the most frequently occurring noun compounds in this volume—*fundraising*—is itself a consequence of understanding MORE in terms of UP. In fact, examination of the evidence suggests that the central metaphor for understanding how all economies work on both large scales and small is the MORE IS UP/LESS IS DOWN metaphor.

Ontological metaphor

Ontological metaphors are metaphors that permit us to understand our experiences of things as disparate as activities like walking or singing and emotions such as anger or love in terms of objects and substances. Among ontological metaphors, the one that seems most relevant for this discussion is the STATES ARE LOCATIONS, or CONTAINER metaphor (for example, "go into debt" or "be in trouble"). This metaphor enables us to understand a society partially as a container with a central area of health, wealth, and vitality, and peripheral or marginal areas of less wealth and lesser opportunity. It also helps us to understand a community in terms of inclusion and exclusion, with members on the inside and nonmembers on the outside. Several of the volumes included on the Indiana University Center on Philanthropy publications list (1996) employ this metaphor. Note, for example, the following (partial) titles: Minorities and *Marginality;* Social *Exclusion;* New Voices at the *Center:* Strengthening the Commitment to an *Inclusive* Society.

Structural metaphor

Structural metaphors are those where the entities of one domain, say that of a journey, correspond to and help us understand the entities of another, more abstract domain, say that of a long-term project to raise money. In the RAISING MONEY IS A JOURNEY metaphor, we understand that, for example, the fundraisers are the travelers embarking on a campaign, their destination is the goal of collecting a certain sum of money, impediments to travel are difficulties for the fundraisers, and so on. The journey metaphor, which can help structure any long-term purposeful activity, is evident in the texts analyzed in the papers gathered for this collection. Again the Indiana University Center on Philanthropy publications list is illustrative: Corporate Philanthropy at the *Crossroads; Toward* a Stronger Voluntary Sector; Our Shared Future: We Must *Get There* Together; The *Quest* for Social Relevance.

Moral accounting

What seems to be the basic underlying conceptual metaphor for the domain of philanthropy, however, is the system of metaphor we have in English for morality. Taken together, this set of metaphors has been labeled "moral accounting" or "moral arithmetic" by Mark Johnson (1993) and George Lakoff (1993).

This complex of metaphor, like all conceptual metaphor, has a nonmetaphorical basis in everyday human experience. Lakoff claims in *Moral Politics* (1996) that the following concepts form our basic experiential and nonmetaphorical understanding of well-being. These conditions provide grounding for our system of moral metaphors. Other things being equal, Lakoff suggests that you are better off if you are healthy rather than sick, rich rather than poor, strong rather than weak, free rather than imprisoned, cared for rather than uncared for, happy rather than sad, whole rather than lacking, clean rather than filthy, beautiful rather than ugly, functioning in the light rather than in the dark, able to stand upright rather than unable to do so, living in a community with social ties rather than in a hostile or isolated one (1996, pp. 41–42).

The moral accounting metaphor finds its fullest articulation in Mark Johnson's book *Moral Imagination* (1993). The metaphor is structured as a complex of transactions and the balance of credits and debits as illustrated in the following list (see pp. 46–47):

Deeds-states are objects in transactions:
   I'm *getting* help from him.
   In return for our kindness, she *gave* us nothing but trouble.
Well-being is wealth:
   I've had a *rich* life.
   Her life has been *impoverished* by her illness.
Moral account is record of transactions:
   Before you judge him, *take into account* all the difficulties he has had.

I'm holding you *accountable* for this mess.
His despicable lying *counts against him in my book.*
Moral balance is balance of transactions:
    One good turn *deserves* another.
    His good deeds *outweigh* his bad ones.
Doing moral deeds is accumulating credit:
    We all *owe* you so much for what you have done.
    She deserves *credit* for all her hard work.
Benefiting from moral deeds is accumulating debt:
    I *owe* you my life.
    He is *indebted* to her for her help.
Doing immoral deeds is accumulating debt:
    He *owes a debt to society* for his crimes.
    We all have to *pay* for our mistakes.

Johnson (1993) credits Sarah Taub and an unpublished UC Berkeley manuscript with identifying five schemas based on the moral accounting metaphor:

1. *Reciprocation:* "One good turn deserves another."
   Event: A gives something good to B.
   Judgment: B owes something good to A.
   Expectation: B should give something good to A.
   Moral inferences: A has a right to receive something good from B.
   Examples: I *owe you* a favor for that good deed. You saved my life; how can I ever *repay* you? You've been so kind; I am deeply *indebted.*
2. *Retribution:* "You'll get yours."
   Event: A gives something bad to B.
   Judgment: B owes something bad to A.
   Expectation: B should give something bad to A.
   Moral inferences: A has an obligation to receive something bad from B.
   Examples: I'll *pay you back* for what you did to me. I *owe you one* for that insult. You'll *get what you deserve* for that.

3. *Restitution:* "I'll make up for it."

   Event: A gives something bad to B.

   Judgment: A owes something good to B.

   Expectation: A should give something good to B.

   Moral inferences: B has the right to receive something good from A.

   Examples: You *owe me* an apology for your rudeness. How can I *pay you* for the damage I have caused? That one mistake *cost me* years of suffering.

4. *Revenge:* "An eye for an eye."

   Event: A gives something bad to B.

   Judgment: A owes something good to B.

   Complication: A will not give something good to B.

   Expectation: B should take something good from A.

   Moral inferences: B has the right to receive something good from A.

   Examples: I'll *make you pay for* what you did. I'll *take it out of your hide.* He'll *get even with you* for this.

5. *Altruism or charity:* "What a saint."

   Event: A gives something good to B.

   Judgment: B owes something good to A.

   Complication: B cannot give something good to A in return. A does not expect B to do so.

   Expectation: A accumulates a certain moral credit in general but expects no concrete good in return.

   Moral inferences: A has gone beyond what is normally required and expected of us.

   Examples: She's a saint—she never expects anything for what she does. I can't understand how he can be so selfless—all that giving without anything in return.

The last schema, altruism, seems to underlie the basic assumptions that one must have (or fundraisers need to foster or instill) in order for funds to be offered to causes that provide no material paybacks. Note that those making the appeals for charity represented in the corpus examined here apparently felt a need to offer at least some return for the generosity asked for. The hypothetical givers appealed to in the letters examined receive thanks, and calls for God's blessings; they are promised tax deductions, and membership privileges.

In the following paragraphs, the metaphors introduced earlier are illustrated with reference to the language found in materials seeking help for Purdue's BCC and in an appeal on behalf of Habitat for Humanity.

BCC (inclusion, well-being, journey)

- *Giant steps*
- *Toward* a new BCC at Purdue University
- Purdue can be a lonely place. For me, the BCC made Purdue feel more like *home*
- The BCC is a cultural treasure that *enriches our* community
- The BCC is for *all of us*

Habitat for Humanity (inclusion)

- We labor alongside other volunteers to build simple, decent *homes in partnership* with people in need
- Just last year, Jimmy and I *joined* with other Habitat *partners*
- What we extend to people is *not a giveaway*
- We work *side-by-side with future homeowners*
- Inviting you to *join us*
- Will you become *partners* with us?
- New *friends*
- Those resources must come from *folks* like you

Finally, although a number of minor metaphors are included in the titles listed in the Indiana University Center on Philanthropy publications list, one that bears mention is related to Lakoff's morality as nurturance metaphor (1996, p. 108) in which the community is a family, moral agents are nurturing parents, and moral action is nurturance:

- *Cultivating* a critical compassion
- *Nurturing* the roots of philanthropy

- The religious *roots* of philanthropy
- *Creating* civil communities
- *Making* me a man that can *stand for the right*

Conclusions

This chapter has introduced a theoretical framework for exploring the use of conceptual metaphor in language and offered an initial and partial description of some of the more obvious metaphors that appear in a small corpus of philanthropic texts. The attempt here has been to raise consciousness among fundraising practitioners about the role that metaphor plays in their discourse. Obviously, a more thorough examination of a much larger sampling of texts is needed before generalizations can be confidently offered. Moreover, in order for fundraisers to begin to incorporate metaphor more effectively into their appeals, an evaluation of which metaphors present their arguments in the most favorable lights must be conducted. Perhaps this chapter will serve as a springboard for further investigations into what metaphors fundraisers "live by" and might live better by.

References

Johnson, M. *Moral Imagination.* Chicago: Chicago University Press, 1993.

Lakoff, G. *Women, Fire, and Dangerous Things: What Categories Reveal About the Mind.* Chicago: University of Chicago Press, 1987.

Lakoff, G. "The Contemporary Theory of Metaphor." In A. Ortony (ed.), *Metaphor and Thought.* (2nd ed.) Cambridge: Cambridge University Press, 1993.

Lakoff, G. *Moral Politics.* Chicago: Chicago University Press, 1996.

Lakoff, G., and Johnson, M. *Metaphors We Live By.* Chicago: University of Chicago Press, 1980.

Lakoff, G., and Turner, M. *More Than Cool Reason: A Field Guide to Poetic Metaphor.* Chicago: University of Chicago Press, 1989.

Langacker, R. *Foundations of Cognitive Grammar.* Vol. 2: *Descriptive Application.* Stanford, Calif.: Stanford University Press, 1991.

PETER MCCAGG *is professor of English at International Christian University, Tokyo, Japan.*

Effective grant proposal writers in nonprofits report that they write differently depending on their organization's relationship with the grant-making organization, distinguishing between proposals written for a familiar local funding source and those written for a more distant source.

4

How writers in nonprofit organizations develop grant proposals

Molly Flaherty Haas

WITH THE SUPPORT of the Indiana University Center on Philanthropy, I am studying the composition of grant proposals in two nonprofit organizations: one, a shelter for homeless families, and the other, a community theater group. Staff members at these nonprofits have generously shared their time to tell me about how they write grant proposals and have also shared some of their successful proposal documents. Before reporting my preliminary findings, I must express a caution about generalizing the findings. Even before beginning this study, I had been studying grant proposal writing in five other nonprofit organizations for several years. Those earlier studies taught me that each organization is unique, and this study reminds me that each proposal is unique even within a single organization. These examples are offered not as models for imitation

NEW DIRECTIONS FOR PHILANTHROPIC FUNDRAISING, NO. 22, WINTER 1998 © JOSSEY-BASS PUBLISHERS

but as creations that suggest interesting things about the practices by which they were made.

Participating organizations

The two organizations in this study are similar in that each has an annual budget of more than a million dollars and several paid full-time staff members. Both have been established for some time. The shelter is a fifteen-year-old organization in a medium-size midwestern city and provides more than eight thousand "shelter nights" per year to families and individual women. The theater has served a small midwestern city for more than fifty years. It presents about a dozen plays a year and also provides classes in acting and theater arts for adults and children. Neither agency relies primarily on grants for support, but directors of both describe grants as a significant source of support.

Grant proposal composing process

Planning and writing grant proposals is an essential part of the administrative work of these organizations at the workplaces I visited. At each, the primary grant proposal writer is a full-time staff member with many other duties. The primary writer works with other staff by gathering information from them, and then having them read drafts of the proposals in order to make suggestions. Many researchers in the field of workplace writing have observed that this kind of collaboration is complicated and influential (for example, Cross, 1994; Dautermann, 1996; Smart, 1993). Coworkers are the first readers of the proposals and participate actively in shaping them, even when only one writer composes the actual sentences.

Agency files are another important source of information for grant proposals. At both workplaces, the writers report reading through and getting ideas from previous grant proposals and other promotional materials. Significantly, they told me that they usually do not import actual sections of text from other proposals into the narrative sections of new proposals. Although they use standard mission statements and other attachments, they choose to compose the narrative sections fresh for each proposal. This strategic decision allows the writers to select and arrange their material to establish a particular relationship within each grant proposal.

Categories of grant proposals

Staff members from both places divided their grants into two different types. They said that their composing methods differ according to whether "small" or "big" grants are being sought. In conversations with proposal writers in my earlier studies, the same distinction between small and big had been common, so I decided to inquire how the writers used this convenient but imprecise distinction. Staff members described small grants as the most common and said they are small in that they require a smaller investment of staff time (commonly a day or so of actual writing and a single reading by other staff) and yield smaller amounts of money. This will not be true everywhere, but at the places I visited the sample small grants have other characteristics in common: they are from local sources, other nonprofits, with which relationships already exist, and they are for specific, concrete goals related to existing programs. The big grants that the participants shared with me are very different. Each takes a week or more of the main writer's time and goes through numerous readings by other staff and board members. These proposals require supporting documentation, including, in the shelter's case, letters of support and clearances from other community agencies. Both of the sample big grants are from "out-of-town" sources, government agencies; they were sought to enable larger program goals rather than particular, concrete purchases.

Relationship suggested in the proposal documents

As a specialist in rhetoric, I look at how—with the goal of persuading—these writers position their organizations in relation to the grant-making organizations in their grant proposal narratives. Writers work in a complicated situation. The total reality of each organization and of the project at hand is more than can be conveyed even in a large grant proposal document. Writers select which details to include and how to express them within the parameters of the grantor's requirements, based on their specialized knowledge of their group and influenced by their perception of their group's relationship with the grantor. This negotiation of relationship in proposal writing has been explored by researchers in both academic and nonprofit settings (for example, Myers, 1990; Connor, 1998; Van Nostrand, 1996). The narrative sections of these small and large sample grants show signs of the writers' awareness of relationship.

Sample small grants

The community theater successfully applied for a grant of about $1,000 from a small local foundation for individual amplification devices for hearing-impaired members of the audience. The homeless shelter received a grant of about $4,000 from a local church to put new flooring in several rooms. In both successful proposals, the writers seem to be addressing readers with whom they already have a connection. They appeal to the existing relationship and shared place and describe the concrete project rather than explicitly describe their organizations.

The theater grant proposal is three pages in all, with slightly more than a single page of narrative, beginning as follows:

[The Theater] is requesting $986 from [the Foundation] to purchase a [Company Name] personal hearing system for use at the theater. This system is designed to provide audience members who are hard of hearing with a personal receiver which is equipped with headphones. The personal receiver accepts and amplifies sounds on the stage through the main transmitter, providing each user with a clear signal.

[The Theater] has a significant number of senior citizens as season ticket holders and patrons. Many individuals have requested that such a system be installed. [comparison with another local venue's system] Installation will enable [the Theater] to provide seven patrons with a personal receiver for each performance. This arrangement will increase the enjoyment of individuals who are hard of hearing while attending plays and musicals. It will also reduce the disturbances caused by individuals who talk amongst themselves trying to piece together what has been said on stage.

The shelter proposal totals three pages, also with only one page of narrative, beginning as follows:

[The Shelter] proposes to install new vinyl flooring in up to four bedrooms used as sleeping quarters for homeless families. The current flooring is carpeting which has been worn and spotted by the many families which have used these rooms. The carpet covers vinyl which is old and very worn. New vinyl flooring will allow us to wash the floor regularly for cleanliness and safety, especially when children spill things or have accidents. Because of the heavy use and the changing population with children of varying ages, we use the heavier grade of flooring for maximum durability.

Like the foundation proposal Ulla Connor studied (1998), which came from an organization of similar size and was also directed to a local nonprofit, both these opening narratives are straightforward. There seems to be an assumption that the competency of the grant-seeking organization is already established. There is a sort of intimacy, an expectation that the reader at the granting organization will recognize familiar, lived experiences: being at the theater when people "talk amongst themselves trying to piece together what has been said on stage," or being at home and responsible for cleaning "worn and spotted carpeting" at times "when children spill things or have accidents." These vivid, informally expressed details seem to fit readers who will recognize a concrete local problem and be ready to help the writer's group solve it without much additional persuasion. In the shelter grant, this theme of working together is emphasized even more. In response to a specific prompt from the granting agency, there is an opening in the proposal document itself for hands-on volunteer help as well as monetary help: "Volunteers are needed to take apart the bunk beds and remove all furniture from each room before the flooring can be installed. . . . Volunteers would also be needed to move the furniture back into the rooms and reassemble the bunk beds."

In both these samples, readers are positioned in close relationship with grant-seeking agencies, who are trusted to be familiar with them, their local situation, and even the specific lived experience of staff and clients.

Sample big grants

In the sample proposals for big grants, in contrast, the relationship seems more formal. The readers are positioned at a greater distance. Both proposals are addressed to government agencies. The readers occupy the position of strangers, knowledgeable about the field in which the grant-seeking agency works but needing to be introduced to the particular agency. Unlike the small grant proposals, each big proposal provides specific information about the group's history and mission as well as describing the proposed project. Just as the amounts requested are big, both proposal documents are big. The theater proposal totals nineteen pages, including seven pages of narrative. The shelter proposal totals fifty-two pages, with fourteen pages of narrative.

Both sample proposals were successful. The theater applied for $20,000 and received $2,000 from a state arts agency to increase staff. The shelter applied for $72,000 and received the full amount from a federal housing agency to start a transitional housing program for families ready to leave the shelter.

For purposes of comparison with the preceding small grant passages, let's look at the sections of narrative in the big proposals in which specific uses of the money are referred to. In the theater proposal, the first reference comes after a general description of the theater group's mission, governance, financial status, and past programming in Section Five: Goals and Activities: "Funds from [State Agency] will enable [Theater] to expand our staff (which is desperately needed) and to expand our programming. Activities will essentially be the same as previous years (although many activities will be expanded in scope) and are clearly outlined in the Past Programming section of this narrative."

A glance back at the Past Programming section shows this reference: "[Theater] also offers a Summer Day Camp, where students ages eight to eighteen participate in full-day workshops for an entire week. Last summer, a second session was added to meet the demand for enrollment."

The last reference is in Section Eleven: Use of [State Agency] Funds and Contingency Plan: "[State Agency] funds will be used to partially fund the salary of our Administrative Assistant/Development Coordinator. This position has been expanded from part- to full-time. [State Agency] funds will also be used to pay the salaries of the assistants we hope to hire during our Summer Day Camp. Finally, [State Agency] funds will be used to pay our adult acting class instructors."

All these sections are more formal than the descriptions in the small grants, and they lack evocations of the actual experience of staff or those who use the agency's services.

An interesting example of the intertwining of the small and large grant applications can be seen in the two theater examples. In the small grant proposal, the personal hearing system was presented as needed immediately by specific persons in the theater: "This arrangement will increase the enjoyment of individuals who are hard of hearing while attending plays and musicals. It will also reduce the disturbances caused by individuals who talk amongst themselves trying to piece together what has been said on stage."

The same listening devices are described in the large grant application as meeting the legal or formal need of both the grant-seeking agency and the government agency for proof of compliance with the Americans with Disabilities Act (ADA): "The Theater is fully accessible to patrons with handicaps, and meets all Federal ADA requirements. . . . The Theater recently purchased a Personal Hearing Assistance monitor which includes six receivers for patrons with hearing impairments."

Thus, the small proposal's "individuals who talk amongst themselves" have become "patrons with handicaps." The writer's selection of which aspect of the hearing assistance devices to emphasize for each reader position seems to be rhetorically effective. Just as the formal mention of compliance with ADA might be expected to interest a government agency, the reference to patrons talking during the show might interest the local foundation readers who have probably attended plays in that very theater.

The shelter's large grant proposal includes six narrative sections. Like the theater, it too includes material to introduce the agency to a reader without local knowledge. The transitional housing project is mentioned in all six sections, and a great deal of supporting detail is included, but it is not of the shared experience variety seen in the small grant proposals. The first reference to the new project is at the end of the Agency Description: "Because of the trust that develops, former residents sometimes contact the shelter for help with new problems or to report successes."

This leads into Purpose of Application: "[Shelter] hopes to expand the continuum of care provided to homeless families by working with some families after they leave the shelter to help them maintain housing stability and strive for self-sufficiency. The first three to six months after a family moves into permanent housing are difficult for families as they adjust their needs to limited income and as they look for or try to keep a job while juggling other priorities."

The Organizational Profile section includes a list of underlying problems with which formerly sheltered families might need help: "money mismanagement, emotional problems or problems within the family, recent family breakup, a family history of domestic abuse or substance abuse, and limited education and job skills."

These sections supply appropriate detail for the agency while remaining formal, as is appropriate for the knowledgeable but remote reader position.

Conclusions

The grant proposal writers in my study choose to compose narratives specifically for each grant, accommodating the variations of possible reader positions in subtle ways that can only be suggested by the few concrete examples included here. Although they themselves do not describe their choices in rhetorical terms, they seem to be practicing effective rhetorical strategies.

Examining small and large grants together reveals that they are sometimes related in a practical way. Participants report that soliciting small local grants can sometimes seem like a burden to overworked staff members who wonder if the money awarded justifies the investment in time and energy. This study suggests that pursuing small grants serves another function besides just financing specific expenditures: the grant proposal process contributes to relationships with both the local community and the big grantors. For example, the shelter's relationship with the church that bought the flooring has continued, with an invitation to the shelter to exhibit at an information fair, the opportunity to recruit volunteers, and explicit recognition by the church of an ongoing connection. This congregation is positioned to support future large and small grant applications by the shelter. When the readers of large grant proposals are far away—as they often are—they need evidence that the applicant organization is supported by local groups near enough to know the agency directly, not just through a proposal document, and a history of successful applications for small, local grants can be a part of the evidence.

The process of writing proposals for large grants can also bring benefits other than the financial support. Participants in this study describe a collaborative proposal writing process that involves multiple staff members and board members and both a proposal document and new developments in the relationships of the staff with the organization. When the grant will enable a significant change in the core programs of the agency, as in the shelter example, the collaborative process provides an opportunity for more members of the group to examine and participate in shaping the change. The power of such day-to-day writing work to play a part in larger changes in an organization has been researched by Bazerman (1994), Myers (1990), and Berkenkotter and Huckin (1995), among others.

These preliminary results offer suggestions about how grant proposal writers do their work and how that work influences dynamic, ever-changing nonprofit organizations. I look forward to future research on the part that writing plays in the relationships of nonprofit organizations and their supporters.

References

Bazerman, C. *Constructing Experience.* Carbondale: Southern Illinois University Press, 1994.

Berkenkotter, C., and Huckin, T. A. *Genre Knowledge in Disciplinary Communication: Cognition, Culture, Power.* Hillsdale, N.J.: Erlbaum, 1995.

Connor, U. M. "Comparing Research and Not-for-Profit Grant Proposals." In *Written Discourse in Philanthropic Fundraising: Issues of Language and Rhetoric.* (Working papers of a conference of the Indiana University Center on Philanthropy.) Indianapolis: Indiana Center for Intercultural Communication and Indiana University Center on Philanthropy, 1998.

Cross, G. A. *Collaboration and Conflict: A Contextual Exploration of Group Writing and Positive Emphasis.* Skokie, Ill.: Rand McNally, 1994.

Dautermann, J. "Social and Institutional Power Relationships in Studies of Workplace Writing." In P. Mortensen and G. E. Kirsch (eds.), *Ethics and Representation in Qualitative Studies of Literacy.* Urbana, Ill.: NCTE, 1996, pp. 241–259.

Myers, G. *Writing Biology: Texts in the Social Construction of Scientific Knowledge.* Madison: University of Wisconsin Press, 1990.

Smart, G. "Genre as Community Invention: A Central Bank's Response to Its Executives: Expectations as Readers." In R. Spilka (ed.), *Writing in the Workplace: New Research Perspectives.* Carbondale: Southern Illinois University Press, 1993.

Van Nostrand, A. D. *Fundable Knowledge: The Marketing of Defense Technology.* Hillsdale, N.J.: Erlbaum, 1996.

MOLLY FLAHERTY HAAS *is a doctoral candidate and teaching assistant in the Rhetoric and Composition Program in the Department of English at Purdue University, West Lafayette, Indiana. She has written successful grant proposals in both nonprofit and industrial settings.*

This chapter presents a study of how six Latino nonprofits that had been taught about generic strategies and prototypical proposal forms formulated their proposals and adapted to the funders' expectations.

5

Language use in grant proposals by nonprofits: Spanish and English

Ulla Connor, Lilya Wagner

A GRANT PROPOSAL can be considered a significant representation of persuasive writing. Its primary purpose is to persuade proposal reviewers and grant agency officials to fund the proposal. Because of this persuasive purpose, grant proposals have a great deal in common with promotional materials such as sales letters and job applications, in which the purpose is to sell a product: in sales letters, a service or product; in letters of application, a person's abilities; in grant proposals, a fundable idea. The linguist Vijay Bhatia (1993) has shown cross-culturally in sales letters and applications that grant proposals need to present a captivating idea, then describe the idea (rhetorical logos), adjust to the needs of the readers (pathos), and establish the writer's competence (ethos).

In this chapter, we investigate how grant proposals for Latino nonprofits are organized. This issue is important to consider both academically and socially. Academically, proposal variations could show differences in rhetoric or culture; socially, the Latino causes

NEW DIRECTIONS FOR PHILANTHROPIC FUNDRAISING, NO. 22, WINTER 1998 © JOSSEY-BASS PUBLISHERS

are in dire need of funding, and so studying proposals may lead to an understanding of the elements necessary to secure funding. Thus, this study attempts to look at the structure, awareness of audience, and presentation of identity in proposals written for Latino nonprofit organizations.

Grant proposal writing

Several linguists and rhetoricians have studied the writing of grant proposals for research funds in particular. Rhetorician Greg Myers (1991, p. 41) has described fundraising as "the most basic form of scientific writing," and he points out that "the researchers must get money in the first place if they are to publish articles and popularizations, participate in controversies, and be of interest to journalists." Following Myers's lead, other researchers have focused on proposal writing in a number of settings using a variety of linguistic and rhetorical frameworks, such as genre analysis and structured systems approach.

In research that examines proposals for European Union research funds, Connor and others (1995) and Connor and Mauranen (in press) have developed a linguistic-rhetorical system of "moves" to describe and evaluate grant proposals. The moves in that system are based on the theory of genre analysis, as proposed by the linguist John Swales (1990): "Genre comprises a class of communicative events, the members of which share some set of communicative purposes" (p. 58). Important in Swales's definition is the centrality of a discourse community whose members agree on the acceptable features of specific genres. According to Swales, research articles, presentations, and grant proposals all represent different genres because their sets of communicative purposes are different. Prototypical "moves," or functional components, can be identified for each genre, which can be taught to a novice writer of a particular genre. Exhibit 5.1 defines the prototypical set of moves for grant proposals.

Exhibit 5.1. A definition of moves

Territory establishes the situation in which the activity in the proposal is placed or physically located. There are two types of territory: that of the "real world" and that of the field of research in which the proposal itself takes place.

Gap indicates that there is a gap in knowledge or a problem in the territory, whether in the real world (ESL/EFL teaching or administration) or in the research field (for example, pointing out that something is not known or certain). This move serves to explain the motivation of the study.

Goal is the statement of aim, or general objective of the proposed activity. In other words, it explains what it is the proposer wants to get done.

$Means_1$ includes the methods, procedures, plans of action, and tasks that the proposal specifies as leading to the goal (that is, procedures of the research or other proposed activity).

$Means_2$ includes the methods and procedures to carry out the actual presentation.

Reporting previous research refers to text that reports on or refers to earlier research in the field, either by the proposing researcher or by others.

Achievements describes the anticipated results, findings, or outcomes of the study or other proposed activity.

Benefits explains the intended or projected outcomes which could be considered useful to the real world outside the study itself, or even outside of the research field.

Competence claim contains statements to the effect that the proposer is well qualified, experienced, and generally capable of carrying out the tasks set out.

Importance claim presents the proposal, its objectives, anticipated outcomes, or the territory as particularly important or topical, much needed or urgent with respect to either the real or research worlds.

Source: Adapted from Connor and others (1995) and Connor and Mauranen (in press).

Connor (1998) compares the use of moves in a proposal written by a small nonprofit organization with the moves used in a research proposal submitted to the National Science Foundation at a university. This study found a difference in the type of moves used; the nonprofit proposal—a seven-page proposal requesting $6,000 from a local foundation—included only territory, goals, means, competence claim, and gap moves, whereas the research proposal—a fifty-two-page document requesting $159,000—used all the grant proposal moves.

It is reasonable to expect that a research proposal submitted to private foundations would include similar moves to the ones found in Connor and Mauranen's study of research grants, yet there are interesting differences according to Connor (1998). Research grant proposals tend to follow a "scientific" style, with moves similar to those found in scientific research articles, and focus heavily on benefits and achievements moves, which make the proposal strong in the eyes of the funder because they show how others outside the proposal writer's organization will benefit from the proposed project. In contrast, the foundation proposal focuses on the goals and means and does not include benefits and achievements. It is imperative that even a proposal written by a small nonprofit discuss the outcomes.

Another theoretical framework—genres as structured systems—has been advanced by rhetorician Charles Bazerman (1994). He locates genres in a system of "complex literate activity constructed through typified actions—typified so that we are all to some extent aware of the form and force of these typified actions" (p. 79). As we become more informed about these literate actions, we learn how texts interact and shape meanings in relation to complex social systems. Grant makers provide grant guidelines, which are read and interpreted by grant proposal writers. Grant proposal writers communicate not only with proposals but also with cover letters and other inquiries—written and spoken—related to their proposal writing. Thus, the actions surrounding a grant proposal involve the communication of various kinds of texts by various kinds of people.

An excellent analysis of grant proposal writing as such a social, literate action is presented in Van Nostrand (1994). Van Nostrand describes a structured system for producing knowledge within the U.S. government's sponsorship of military research and development. His analyses show that many recursive cycles of negotiated knowledge take place between the vendors (that is, university laboratories) and the U.S. Department of Defense. In other words, vendors and the government negotiate about the need and the solution over a period of time in the process of proposal writing. Van

Nostrand writes: "Rhetorically, the R&D project culminates a history of negotiation that has proceeded in stages by means of a discourse exchange system. The documents exchanged by customer and vendor define the objectives, budget, and duration of the project by iterating the activities that will comprise it. These iterations progressively shape the project and define the deliverable knowledge products that the project is intended to generate" (p. 135).

Van Nostrand documents seven different genres as part of the proposal writing process in this research: four initiated by the customer, such as request for proposal and broad agency announcement, and three initiated by the vendor, such as white paper and proposal. Van Nostrand finds that even these genres are generic with variations in prototypicality according to the writer's sense of the audience expectations. He writes: "There is a startling difference in register between the vendor's proposal, which is categorically responsive to the reader's expectations, and the customer's RFP, which has all the sensitivity of a landlord's contract" (p. 141).

The two sets of writers and readers in Van Nostrand's study had different basic communicative needs: customers and vendors convey their needs through different subsets of genres. They participate cooperatively in the same genre system, in a negotiation of transactional documents that entails a reciprocity. Starting from different perspectives, they come together in defining a feasible research project. The project gains a fixed, shared purpose.

Van Nostrand's research sets up a useful framework for analyzing the proposal writing process in nonprofits, identifying it as a structured system with writers and readers that may, in fact, conflict. In the case of government R&D grants, the process of negotiation develops a common communicative purpose. However, in the case of research and nonprofit proposals, as Connor and Mauranen's (in press) and Connor's (1998) research shows, there often is not such an intensive process of negotiation about the common goals. In these cases, the grant proposal writer has more responsibility. According to Van Nostrand, he or she is in the position of a seller who needs to know what exactly the buyer wants.

Relatively little research has been done on grant proposal writing in nonprofits. For this chapter, we wanted to collect and analyze more proposals from nonprofits than in Connor (1998). In addition, we were interested in cross-cultural aspects of proposal writing. Each of us brought an interest in cross-cultural differences in communication as well as a second-language speaker's background into this research. Our project includes expertise in fundraising and fundraising training (Wagner) and linguistics (Connor).

The importance of identity

An important aspect of writing deals with how writers represent themselves in their writing, how they express their identities, and how they reconcile conflicts between what they might ideally want and the constraints imposed by conventions. Writer identity has been discussed by Clark and Ivanic (1997), who propose the following four elements in the constitution of writer identity: clarifying one's commitment to one's ideas, deciding how to take responsibility, masking or declaring one's own position, and establishing one's own sociopolitical identity as a writer.

Thus, writing not only conveys a message about content but also conveys a message about the writer. The term *self-representation* refers to this process, which is partly dependent on one's life history, experiences and affiliations to a particular group, and partly on the pressure to conform to the genre conventions in the institutional context.

The conscious or subconscious selections that writers make from among possibilities for selfhood are based on their assessment of the characteristics of the immediate social context. This involves understanding both the purpose of the particular writing they are engaged in and the nature of the reader-writer relationship they are entering into. Writers have to make judgments about the power relations between themselves and their readers; this presentation of self depends on whether it is necessary for writers to maintain good standing in the eyes of the readers or whether they can afford to ignore the impressions of them that their readers might form.

The model assumes both that genres have ideological constructs and that the conventions associated with them are never monolithic but rather the object of a considerable amount of struggle (Clark and Ivanic, 1997). Individual writers may employ prototypical genre conventions but they may also decide to alter the prototypical genre models for their own purposes, such as establishing special identity.

Latinos and U.S. philanthropic fundraising

The designation *Hispanic* is used by the U.S. Bureau of the Census to describe persons in the United States who were born in Spanish-speaking Latin American countries or Spain or who can trace their ancestry to these countries. Subsuming all Spanish-speaking population groups under one rubric is a highly sensitive matter. The Latino presence in the United States includes not only a variety of nationalities but also subgroups with racial, religious, linguistic, ethnic, and socioeconomic differences. Recent objectors to the term Hispanic view the label as referring only to the Spanish European legacy within Latino communities. Thus, many prefer the term *Latino*, which denotes Latin American (by contrast with North American) origin and is more inclusive. For that reason, we generally use the term Latino rather than Hispanic in this chapter.

There are twenty-two million Latinos in the United States. By the year 2000 the numbers may reach thirty-one million. By the year 2005, Latinos will become our largest ethnic minority. At present, the United States is the fifth largest Latino country in the world. Yet in spite of their numbers, Latinos are known as the invisible minority. This is certainly true when it comes to fundraising and philanthropy by and for Latinos.

Until recently, organized philanthropy in the United States has largely ignored Latino population groups. In the early 1990s, foundation giving to Latino causes and communities was only 1.4 percent of all grants. This is only a 0.4 percent increase over giving in 1980. The depth of need in Latino causes has led philanthropic organizations to expand their attention to include organizations and practices relevant to growing minority populations. Yet there is a dearth of funds; money allotted to Latino causes is scarce. Nevertheless, proposals for funding have been increasing from Latino organizations as a strategy for seeking support for their causes.

The study

The research questions in this study are these: (1) What are the steps in the process of proposal writing? (2) What level of understanding do the writers have of their potential funders' goals and purposes in funding? Specifically, did the writers express awareness of audience, and did they contain proposal "moves" such as ones included in the Hispanic Stewardship Development Partnership training? (3) How do the proposals exhibit the Latino self-identity of the organizations and the writers?

Materials

The seven proposals studied in this project were prepared and written by Latino personnel in six different Latino nonprofits in the United States: Southeast Pastoral Institute (SEPI), Mexican American Cultural Center (MACC), National Catholic Council for Hispanic Ministry (NCCHM), Latino Pastoral Action Center, Hispanic Alliance, and Mundelein College.

Each organization had been part of the project entitled the Hispanic Stewardship Development Partnership, which was funded by the Lilly Endowment. The project focuses on fundraising training, development, and implementation in U.S. Latino church and parachurch organizations. As part of the project, the staff from the organizations had attended an intensive two-week training session in fundraising provided by the IU Center on Philanthropy. The training included instruction in proposal writing.

Data analysis

The analyses consisted of textual analyses of the proposals as well as analyses of discourse-based phone interviews with the writers of the proposals. The interviews were conducted in order to understand the intentions of the writers and to assess the degree of negotiation between the writer's organization and the funder in the process of the proposal writing. The interviews were structured around three major questions: the proposal writing process, including questions on proposal authorship, outside assistance on writing and editing, and the number of drafts; reasons for choosing the particular foundation or agency sought as a funder, such as background knowledge on the agency, contact with the agency before and during the writing, and perceptions on why this particular agency might fund; and presentation of the organization's Latino identity, including questions on playing up that identity, masking that identity, and reasons for such choices.

Results

Question 1: Proposal writing process. The interviews revealed that grant proposal writing in each organization is a complex, structured process. Each organization has a person identified as the grant writer, but in each case the grant writer solicits comments on the proposal in its formulation and revision. One writer recounts: "I write it, have several people work on it, two to three people read it to make sure that content, program and development people are in it, for language, clarity." Another writer in a newer, smaller organization states: "I write drafts, consult with the board."

In the two largest organizations, the process between the grant writer and the director of the organization is especially organized. One says: "She writes, I review them, she's a professional in education, bilingual." The other, the writer in another organization, says: "This year is the most we've sent out, five proposals a month. My boss looks at it. My boss tells me his ideas, and I write it. I send it to him. I change."

Each interviewee spoke about the importance of having an Anglo or a bilingual with an Anglo proficiency review proposals for language and punctuation before they are submitted.

Question 2: Audience awareness and use of moves. Each writer interviewed in this study showed a keen awareness of the match between the funder and his or her organization's needs and request. The writers know that the guidelines of the foundations are important to follow: "We read their guidelines." "We follow their directions." "I read what the foundation guidebook says about them, and I'll highlight effects of our work. If I'm writing to a foundation with a focus on Catholic religion, I'll highlight the religious part of our mission, I play up religion. If they are against religion, I'll highlight the effects of our other work, such as socioeconomic improvement." "I am constantly looking for funding sources. Guidelines from them. I match with what they fund. I boilerplate proposals. I highlight things that are of interest to them."

The interviewees acknowledged a heightened awareness about the importance of the relationship with the funder thanks in part to the training they had received in grant proposal writing in the Hispanic Stewardship Development Partnership, saying things like this: "Through our history, we have to learn by ourselves, we learn by doing it, but we learned techniques, we realized that my intuition has been correct for fifteen years, but there were things that I didn't know, for instance, that a funding source should not rest." "We were writing proposals before but it helps us to follow directions from foundation."

The use of discourse features, including the use of moves in the proposals, follows the pattern found in previous research on proposals by native English-speaking writers (Connor and Mauranen, in press; Connor, 1998). There was no identifiable L1 transfer; in fact, writers seemed to go to any lengths necessary to have the proposal seem Anglo, including having the proposals corrected and proofread with the Anglo readers of the foundations in mind. One writer states: "We're aware that we're in the Anglo world; if we write to the Anglo world, we play the game. Since we have Anglo training, we try to be as close to their mentality without betraying our goals and objectives. As direct as possible, as short as possible, only use one word instead of three words."

Question 3: Framing identity in the proposal. We believe that grant proposals are socially ratified literacy practices and that their prototypical forms are teachable, and in fact both of us have taught these forms to novice grant writers, Connor in the academic setting, Wagner in The Fundraising School's training units. Yet previous research on genres (Bazerman, 1994; Clark and Ivanic, 1997) convinces us that genres are not fixed even if certain practices and discourse forms may be dominant.

Furthermore, because successful writers in all situations need to take responsibility, either through masking or declaring their own positions, we expected that the Latino writers represent themselves with some traces of Latino identity. Contrary to an expectation based on contrastive rhetoric theory, there was little evidence of a Latino identity in the organization or its staff except in the identification of the organization (however, this is what proposal writers were taught to do—that is, write to the audience). In most cases, the proposals could have been written by any urban minority organization. One proposal describes its "gap" problem as follows: "The UYFLP [a program of the Latino Pastoral Action Center] has been primarily serving the Latino and black youth population. Our impact is felt both in the community and citywide."

Another writes: "The Latino Pastoral Action Center's mission is to educate, equip, and empower Latino and other urban churches in developing holistic organizations in their communities. In the past four years, we have fulfilled this mission by developing twenty church-based organizations, and providing direct services to more than five thousand congregants."

In most proposals, the only direct reference to Latino sensitivity occurs in a personnel section in statements such as this: "The person occupying this position will preferably have a master's degree in social work or a related field or a bachelor's degree in a human services field and at least five years' experience working with grassroots organizations and community organizing. It is necessary to have a person who is fluent in English and Spanish and

who is sensitive to the nuances of the cultures of the people resid-
ing in the area. Ideally, this person will be a longtime resident of
the Highbridge community, or have a good practical knowledge
of the vicinity."

In response to the interview question about highlighting or
masking Latino identity, we learned that the writers knew that their
readers were Anglo and that relatively few Latino officials were
working in the foundations. As one of the interviewees said, "We
need to play the game—very few Hispanics working in philanthropic fundraising, not a big philanthropic tradition yet."

Another experienced fundraiser spoke about the importance of
"reading" the foundation people: "I would read—are they risk tak-
ers? Are they conservatives? I like to take risks. I like to play down
the new stuff and highlight what they are interested in; if they are
interested in funding people of color, I sometimes just mention the
numbers. I don't like to throw it to their face. I use enough that is
very specific to the target population, but not too much so they
think they are funding a biased group. I don't think that there is a
need to mention the Hispanic identity. There are not Latino organizational models if I need to put that. It depends to whom I'm
writing; most foundations have Anglo employees. You give them
what they want, don't think that you're so special."

When asked why the Latino writers did not employ characteristics identified as cultural traits, a grant proposal writer responded:
"When we talk—face-to-face—we may talk about family aspects,
when one-on-one, but not in writing. We're just as clear as anyone
else. When I work with Protestant organizations, we go ahead and
make close contact and be familiar and make them understand.
Maybe not in writing."

Thus, it would appear from the analyses that the Latino organizations are familiar with their readers' expectations and knowledge and do not want to risk not getting funded by playing up the
Latino background of their organization. It is worth noting, however, that two of the seven proposals play up the Latino identity;
both of these proposals, which were written by two Latinas and
submitted to local organizations in order to facilitate access to

higher education for Latinas, were written in the early 1990s, before the training in philanthropic fundraising and grant proposal writing. Both proposals play up Latinos' special nature and include descriptions of the target populations such as these: "Many Hispanic students are very shy by nature and are fearful of the process of applying for aid. This is due partly to their culture but also may be a by-product of the family's socioeconomic status and/or the lack of early education."

The proposals also include student profiles, which describe in a very vivid manner the life of a typical Latina who would benefit from the funding. It is difficult to say why the two proposals differ so drastically in their rhetorical appeals from the five others in the sample. Perhaps their applying to local agencies made the difference. Perhaps the fact that the writers were not exposed to the training in the truly generic form of grant proposals given to the writers in the sample made the difference. Perhaps the fact that they dared to bring to life the difference of the Latinos made the difference. These are interesting questions.

Conclusions

In this study we examined seven grant proposals written in Latino organizations in the United States. We were interested in the processes of writing and the relationship between the writers and readers. We conducted text analyses and interviewed the writers. There were three major research questions in the study dealing with the process of proposal writing, the relationship between the organizations and foundations, and the representation of the Latino identity in the proposals.

The research showed that the writers have a keen awareness of the match between the funder and the nonprofit's needs and request. There was little evidence that the Latino organizations displayed ethnic identity in the written proposals. It seemed that the organizations were familiar with the Anglo readers' expectations and did not want to risk funding by playing up their ethnic background.

72   THE LANGUAGE OF FUNDRAISING

The study raises issues at many levels. The adherence to the prototypical Anglo expectations by the Latino organizations—although a successful strategy—suggests that at present it is more important for them to maintain good standing in the eyes of the readers. We did not interview the readers, however. Future research should ascertain whether the readers were indeed Anglos as the writers expected and what they thought about the self-representation of the proposal writers.

From the point of view of training in fundraising, the study raises a dilemma. The training in proposal writing provided by the IU Center on Philanthropy to the writers studied offers guidelines about proposals that have been devised by Anglos—the people in power. On the one hand, as is recommended by contrastive rhetoric theory (Connor, 1996; Reid, 1992), writers need to be taught the expectations of their native English-speaking readers. On the other hand, writers should be given choices to adjust their styles depending on the audience. Furthermore, according to recent theories, genres are ideological constructs that are in constant flux. Accordingly, Latino writers should be encouraged to participate in the shaping of the genre and educating their readers about the special circumstances of Latinos in this country. After all, Anglos need to learn to appreciate Latinos more, too. As already noted, by the year 2005, Latinos will make up the largest ethnic minority in this country.

References

Bazerman, C. "Systems of Genres and the Enactment of Social Intentions." In A. Freedman and P. Medway (eds.), *Genre and the New Rhetoric*. London: Taylor and Francis, 1994.

Bhatia, V. K. *Analyzing Genre: Language Use in Professional Settings*. White Plains, N.Y.: Longman, 1993.

Clark, R., and Ivanic, R. *The Politics of Writing*. New York: Routledge, 1997.

Connor, U. *Contrastive Rhetoric: Cross-Cultural Aspects of Second Language Writing*. Cambridge: Cambridge University Press, 1996.

Connor, U. "Comparing Research and Not-for-Profit Grant Proposals." In U. Connor (ed.), *Written Discourse in Philanthropic Fundraising: Issues of Language and Rhetoric*. Indianapolis: Indiana Center on Philanthropy, 1998.

Connor, U., Helle, T., Mauranen, A., Ringbom, H., Tirkkonen-Condit, S., and Yli-Antola, M. *Tehokkaita EU-Projektiehdotuksia. Ohjeita Kirjoittajille*. Helsinki, Finland: TEKES, 1995.

Connor, U., and Mauranen, A. "Linguistic Analysis of Grant Proposals: European Union Research Grants." *English for Specific Purposes Journal*, in press.

Myers, G. "Conflicting Perceptions of Plans for an Academic Centre." *Research Policy*, 1991, *20*, 217–235.

Myers, G. "Centering: Proposals for an Interdisciplinary Research Center." *Science, Technology, and Human Values*, 1993, *18* (4), 433–459.

Reid, J. "A Computer Text Analysis of Four Cohesion Devices in English Discourse by Native and Nonnative Writers." *Journal of Second Language Writing*, 1992, *1* (2), 79–108.

Swales, J. *Genre Analysis: English in Academic and Research Settings.* Cambridge: Cambridge University Press, 1990.

Van Nostrand, A. D. "A Genre Map of R&D Knowledge Production for the U.S. Department of Defense." In A. Freedman and P. Medway (eds.), *Genre and the New Rhetoric.* London: Taylor and Francis, 1994.

ULLA CONNOR *is professor of English and adjunct professor of women's studies and philanthropic studies at Indiana University–Purdue University, Indianapolis, where she directs the Indiana Center for Intercultural Communication.*

LILYA WAGNER *is associate director of public service at the Indiana University Center on Philanthropy and is a faculty member of The Fund Raising School.*

This chapter examines the ways in which visual rhetoric operates in printed documents and in Web documents.

6

Into print, into Webs: The consideration of visual rhetoric for print and on-line philanthropic documents

Patricia Sullivan

IN 1984, only the wealthy had laser printers, no word processing packages could deliver two-column text, and no one could deliver color images without an expensive and lengthy press run. Today, even small operations can get access to advanced layout, imaging, and color printing at a photocopying store (and sometimes at a library). Further, the World Wide Web is quickly developing multimedia delivery opportunities suitable for sophisticated media messages. Every year my students are more digitally involved than before; every year my own job requires more digital work and more print work. Although the digital move does not erase print, or even lessen it, the new digital technology draws writers' attention to the visual and the verbal in new and interesting ways.

This is true in philanthropic settings as well as elsewhere. Today more than ever before, fundraisers need to develop keen awareness of how visual rhetoric operates both in print and in on-line settings.

NEW DIRECTIONS FOR PHILANTHROPIC FUNDRAISING, NO. 22, WINTER 1998 © JOSSEY-BASS PUBLISHERS

Because technology can help writers (and other ordinary people) complete tasks that fifteen years ago would have been done only by highly trained graphic professionals, digital technology has opened the door for fundraisers working for small and large organizations alike to develop Web sites as well as to take over much of the production for printed materials. But that does not mean the print and on-line documents produced by writers unaccustomed to production will overflow with verve or grace. Yes, as writers take more control of the material production of discourse, the need for sensitivity to the ways that the visual carries messages to audiences becomes more acute. We need only remember how the exuberance caused by laser printers and page layout programs led to newsletters with ten typefaces and gratuitous clip art to understand how enthusiasm for technology can defeat graphic design principles.

What dimensions of visual rhetoric have an impact on philanthropic discourse so that writers can work to use them in shaping effective messages to donors? I present the advice professional writing researchers have given to workplace writers about how visual rhetoric operates in printed documents and what they are saying about visual rhetoric and the emergence of Web-based documents. I play the two media off each other because print has a profound influence on professional Web-based communications and because the technology challenges of designing Web-based communication point out the visual maneuvers we work in print. The examples focus the discussion on philanthropic documents in hopes that this chapter airs issues for visual rhetoric that are key for philanthropic discourse.

Visual rhetoric and the printed page

We live in a visual world. Even when text is the focus, as it is in print literacy, visual conventions carry meaning—through tactics such as grouping, emphasizing, and employing or breaking aesthetic rules. Professional writing not only studies how visual rhetoric operates but also attempts to teach writers how to use visual dimensions of texts to their own ends. Thus, you can find authors describing how visual elements of texts operate to carry meaning to readers and also developing guidelines for writers to use in their texts. When they do so, they normally focus on parameters such as these:

- The first analytic language of the visual is aesthetic. But when you want to make aesthetic analysis useful to communicators, it must be massaged to make it rhetorically sensitive. Functional approaches to graphic principles of page design offer insufficient guidance because they focus somewhat dispassionately on composition and not on how audiences receive and respond to the visual. But that does not mean professional writers have abandoned functional approaches. Instead they have built a kind of rhetorical and functional approach that places the user (or reader) at the center of the writer's decisions (Johnson, 1998).
- A visual rhetoric of the page is founded on the grid of a page (Berryman, 1984; Williamson, 1989) as it is traditionally built for each print genre. The guidance for layout, typography, images, color, and so on, are predicated on audiences experiencing visual genres in predictable, culturally influenced ways.
- "Visual" is ambiguous because it refers to the general look of a page, the visual devices aimed at directing readers' attention, and the development and use of visual representations for information (for example, tables, figures, or pictures). Because the visual is more powerful than words for some readers, visual rhetoric focuses on coordinating the visual and the verbal arguments in a print document (Bernhardt, 1986; Barton and Barton, 1987; Porter and Sullivan, 1994).
- Visual rhetoric is not so thoroughly developed that it offers specific advice for specific genres—that is, there are not unique guidelines for proposals or philanthropic documents. Instead, visual rhetoric is sometimes spoken of only as a criticism that flows from readers' sense of visual error or excess. In philanthropic documents this criticism might be expressed obliquely as a "Is this how they are spending my money?" or a "Mighty fancy!" to a visually arresting mailing.

• An organization develops a look for its documents that makes them recognizable as originating from that organization. This image can be limited to a particular fundraising campaign, or it may come to be codified into a style sheet and associated with all documents originating from the organization. Certainly these efforts to standardize the look emanating from an organization become a force in the visual culture shaping a particular document. Other cultural factors that visually shape a document include the samples distributed by a funding agency, the requirements for a proposal, and the look of prize-winning fundraising materials, to name but a few obvious choices.

Visual rhetoric blends an awareness of visual aesthetics with a concern for the needs and wishes of the audience. Such a position is complicated because there is not one visual aesthetic that page designers can follow. Carl Dair ([1967] 1985) points that out in typography by articulating that "design . . . is the art of assembling diverse elements into an organized unit" and then undercutting that simple formula by insisting that the relationships among elements cannot be determined more strictly than by making sure they use and balance the principles of concord and contrast. Donis Dondis, in his *Primer of Visual Literacy* (1973), clarifies the multiple visual aesthetics by organizing them into a continuum of five styles: primitive, expressionistic, classical, embellished, and functional. Dondis argues that these five approaches to the visual emphasize vastly different design aesthetics, with the primitive involving exaggeration, spontaneity, activeness, simplicity, distortion, flatness, irregularity, roundness, and colorfulness, whereas the functional involves simplicity, symmetry, angularity, predictability, consistency, sequentiality, unity, repetition, economy, subtlety, flatness, regularity, sharpness, monochromaticity, and mechanicalness.

Although the visual rhetorics prized by professional writing research have focused on Dondis's category of functional aesthetics, they have added reader (or user) response as critical to making visual design decisions. In doing so, they have made it reasonable to bend the aesthetic to one judged more appropriate for the audience and situation. That melding of visual aesthetics and concern with rhetorical effectiveness for an audience produces visual rhetoric. It also makes visual rhetoric a flexible enough tool to make it attractive to philanthropic writers: it helps in the analysis and structuring of the visual dimensions on fundraising messages.

Marking visual meaning in texts

In print, professional writing has worked to focus writers' visual decision making on deploying visual markers in texts. Much of the interesting work on visual markers in a text has started with an interest in readability, usability, or comprehension: it views the finished text from the reader's perspective, then works backward. Document design research, for example, presents a range of studies showing that visual redesign improves reader comprehension (Redish, 1993; Schriver, 1989). Professional writing pedagogy applies this focus on the reader when it evaluates the visual requirements from the lens of readers' needs. This emphasis is laudable and a necessary critiquing tool, and as such it forms a part of the needed visual theory. But it moves to a writer-centered perspective as it highlights the choices writers make about visual cueing.

Table 6.1 describes three of the approaches aimed at turning knowledge about readers' visual practices into writer actions: the guidelines approach pioneered by American Institutes for Research (AIR), the instructional design decisions approach articulated by James Hartley (1985), and the forging of graphics and human factors into an information-reader model that has been developed by Keyes (1987) and by Keyes, Sykes, and Lewis (1988). These approaches give writers ways to talk about writerly decisions about the placing of visual cues in a text. Though not mutually exclusive, all three approaches have their origins in disparate document design projects. American Institutes for Research has worked in the redesign of consumer forms, whereas Hartley has worked on designing textbooks, and Keyes and Watzman have tackled a classic design task of packaging corporate information. Because the nature of their design problems and tasks differ profoundly, it is not unexpected that their solutions take different views to the writer's task.

Table 6.1. Visual markers used to guide readers through texts

	AIR (*Guidelines*)	Hartley (*Design decisions*)	Watzman/Keyes (*Information-reader model*)
Focal projects	Consumer forms	Textbooks	Corporate information and packaging
Sources for approach	Linguistics; comprehension research	Aesthetics; text design research; readability; educational psychology	Aesthetics; human factors; readability
What writers do about visual meaning	Consult guidelines; consult models	High-level design based on purpose and design problems; evaluation and change	Research a corporation; research readers; build designs; evaluation and change
Visual tactics suggested (listed from easier to harder to produce)	Use highlighting (bold, italic, underline); use line length; use white space; use ragged right margins; avoid all caps; use illustrations to explain; use color and elaborate layout	Margins; line spacing; placing illustrations (near text? captioned? reference in text?); typographic detail (underline, bold, italic, caps); columns; color	Filtering (place on page, easy-to-scan headings, bullets, numbered lists, icons, summary tables); queuing (heading hierarchy, spatial placement, type weight); conceptual maps; queuing (color)

This work dates to at least 1981 when AIR published *Guidelines for Document Designers* (Felker, 1981), a checklist for designing a text. These guidelines gave writers rules of thumb for making reasonable visual choices and avoiding egregious errors. Writers were told, for instance, the range of typefaces and type sizes they should use in constructing readable text. The guidelines proved to be a good initial step. They gave writers who knew nothing about visual design a basic vocabulary and a set of "rules." AIR has continued to pursue this writer's advice approach to visual design with success but has not pushed the guidelines to provide rules for genres or any other larger text frame. Their layout advice usually is communicated through before and after pictures of documents they have redesigned. Hence, the guidelines approach retains the quality of standards and specifications that need to be met.

The design decisions approach is derived from the work of James Hartley (1985), a British designer of instructional text and an educational psychologist. Hartley focuses on the decisions faced by a textbook designer and assumes that the writer will make critical design choices (such as page dimensions, basic page design, use of color and type) at the start of a project. Those decisions will be based on the writer-designer's understanding of how the text will function and how readers will approach the text. Hartley's is a more comprehensive approach than AIR's, as it directly addresses the placement of textual units on the page as well as with qualities of the text itself.

Elizabeth Keyes (1987) mixes human factors with traditional design aesthetics to develop an approach to information design that features the linking of information structures to a reader model. Keyes's approach to visual design focuses on translating a cognitive model of how a reader reads into visual decisions that are made about technical documents. She ties visual techniques for document design to activities that readers perform, such as skimming, ordering, grouping, relating, and accessing information. Writers use an analysis of what activities readers will perform to help them develop a visual logic for placing material onto a page. The advantage of this approach lies with the tying of reader and reading activity to concrete decisions about the design of the page.

Still, these approaches (as well as others operating in the field) are inadequate to handle all the decisions about visual rhetoric. Just as their strength lies with making readers important, their potential weakness lies with making a fixed (and inflexible) model of how readers read the arbiter of visual decisions. In addition to markers, visual rhetoric needs to involve an understanding of the forces shaping the production of a document.

Visual rhetoric and philanthropic documents

So far we have talked about visual rhetoric within the framing of how visual markers can cue meaning for readers and also adding commentary about technology along the way. Although markers are an important reason why visual rhetoric is important to understanding the audience effectiveness of all printed documents, other forces shape documents as well. For example, the forces that shape the visual rhetoric of a philanthropic proposal are likely to include discourse studies, subject, graphic design, technology, and rhetorical situation.

Why are these shaping forces worth our attention? Another aspect of visual rhetoric comes from consideration of the organizational culture surrounding the document produced. In most situations a document's visual rhetoric is shaped by the forces that lead to its production. When I revise the flyer advertising the Graduate Program in Rhetoric and Composition at Purdue, for example, I am conscious of the modest production limits (only color is the paper, ink is black, page size is specified) and the flyer's uses (tacked to bulletin boards at other schools and sent to prospective students). But I am also aware of the external competition for students (most other graduate programs have glossy brochures using color photography and multiple documents for mailings) and the internal competition (my program flyer is sent with other English department flyers and cannot be thought to draw unreasonable attention). Further, Purdue's institutional decision to minimize central funds devoted to marketing means that I cannot successfully request money for a "fancy" brochure or a program mailing. I cannot compete with the money others put into the project and must rely on skilled visual design to make my flyer connect with students who understand how good it is on such a modest budget. Ultimately, I have to structure a message that depicts the graduate program and its mission while working within the forces that shape its production.

When commenting on philanthropic discourse and its shaping forces, Charles Stephens (1998) put it this way: "My cautions, as we seek to develop the philosophical basis for print and electronic visual rhetoric for philanthropy, nonprofits, and fundraising through research, are that we must remain sensitive to what is right and to what is necessary to assure that we connect our audience with our mission. . . . Organizational mission must always be the single most defining factor" (p. 2).

Visual cues and proposals for funding

Let me close the discussion of visual rhetoric for print with an example that illustrates how attention to visual cues operates in a government research proposal on fatty acids. This proposal, a revision that has been resubmitted to the granting agency, is minimal in its use of visual appeal, which makes it typical of most government grant proposals. Yet visual rhetoric is at work in the document. The authors render the original form provided by the granting agency in typeface 1, which they never use for their own words, a move that separates them from the agency (and also allows them to add and subtract space from the form as needed). They also bring typography into focus when they add a note that claims the original text is in typeface 2 and the revised text is in typeface 3. Their typeface note, which follows the introduction, is in typeface 4, leaving the introduction's relation to the project unfixed, at least historically. Much of the background retains the original text, emphasizing that the revision does not qualitatively change the relationship of the project to the original idea and the research that idea spawned. Drawings that explain the theory behind the research remain unchanged as well, suggesting that the theory and its explanation are the same in the original and the revision. Because much of the additional text found in the revision presents findings of studies that are already under way, this visual rhetoric underscores that the research continues and that the findings are mounting. "The funding agency should get onboard!" suggests this typographically underscored rhetoric of the revision. The authors are clearly trying to use typography to direct readers' attention visually even though they are working within the constrained format of a grant application. And their diligence is rewarded because the visual elements underscore some arguments they are making beneath the surface of the words.

It is important to note how control over print technology has affected writers' options in even such a constrained form. In the 1960s, when the grant cover form for this proposal was probably developed, typewriters ruled the office and offered few typographic options (or layout possibilities) for document production. If one wanted to produce print-quality work (that is, a resolution of more than 1200 dpi) or four fonts or advanced layout, such production required a skilled printer, a linotype machine operator, and a hot lead form. Today, sophisticated layout features are available to everyone who uses word processing software, and most office laser printers offer near print-quality production.

Of course, the visual rhetoric of the corporate proposal would operate differently from the example offered by a government grant proposal, as would a direct mail letter to past contributors. The genre, the situation, the relationship invoked by the document— all are important to shaping a writer's decision making about the visual rhetoric of a piece. An appeal from Rosalynn Carter to support Habitat for Humanity could hardly be expected to follow the strict visual conventions of a government research proposal. We would expect such a letter to have a personal insignia and be printed using a typewriter font. We might also expect handwritten emendations (or at least a handwriting font), perhaps in a blue ink that would create visual contrast in type and color. Such a visual approach would square with our images of a former first lady, Southern lady, and public figure so connected to this cause that she would take time to write.

Visual rhetoric and on-line culture

What happens to visual rhetoric when it goes from supporting a print culture to living in an on-line one? Because Web culture is so new, and because we are just beginning to see how profoundly the Web changes writing, we have not yet learned all the questions we must ask about how visual rhetoric operates in on-line cultures. By asking about visual rhetoric from the perspective of philanthropic discourse, we take an important step to understanding visual rhetoric on-line, that is, we particularize the Web's use inside a culture we can understand in other ways so that we may connect the visual to rhetoric.

Since Jay Bolter published *Writing Space* in 1991, hypertext enthusiasts have focused on how hypertext is the way to move past print into on-line writing spaces. Various claims about hypermedia's ability to move us past linearity (Holtzman, 1998), or past print literacy (most), or past modernism (Landow, 1992), focus almost exclusively on text (see Johnson-Eilola's [1997] critique). Further, when theorists become interested in cyberspace, too often they see it as a way to work out their current theories—for example, to build new subjectivities (Haraway, 1997; Terry and Calvert, 1997)—rather than exploring it as a space that is building cultures of its own (though Haraway does exploring as well as experimenting). Although the space offers new ground for philosophy, and that philosophy is a force shaping our understandings of visual rhetoric on-line, in this discussion we need to focus on some of the practical differences between print and on-line cultures as they affect philanthropic discourse.

Visual rhetoric on-line: Shaping forces

Some of the forces shaping visual rhetoric on-line derive from the differences between print and on-line documents (both their production and their aesthetics). The Web's conduciveness to interactivity, animation, and video all work against the stable and static visual aesthetics that have grown to carry meaning on the page.

The more the Web cultures evolve, the more they suggest that the production of writing and the production of Web sites face somewhat different challenges.

Some of the differences result from the document stability issues that are important in Web pages (see the following list). Although instability is woven into the production of print and the Web, print's ability to control the look its page delivers seems comforting in the face of the myriad ways that people can view a Web page across platforms and browsers. Considerable planning is necessary for a Web page to look approximately the same in most environments and accommodate users with lesser technology. Furthermore, the text's content does not vary; it is the visual look of the page that shimmers and shakes.

Print: Stability of Initial View	*Web: Stability of Initial View*
Rhetorical decisions related to money can make a document seem expensive or not (paper, theme logo, color), but once produced, each copy is the same.	Viewing platform variation means that not everyone sees the graphics, animation, fonts, video; text doesn't stay aligned; and colors don't stay stable.
Quality of photocopies degrades.	Quality of digital copies is identical to the original.

Print: Stability over Time	*Web: Stability over Time*
May be difficult to produce, but is stable once printed.	A site viewed at different times may be different because of changes made.

Navigational variations, another major source of difference, result in part from design differences and in part from the different ways that users-readers approach and work through pages and screens (see Figure 6.1). Through centuries of practice, Western

Figure 6.1. Web surface invites a different organization of information and navigation

Book

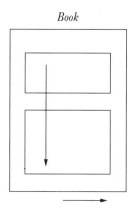

Web Screen

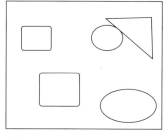

All main content divisions on the surface of the home page

Information written in one path

Visitors choose paths through the site

Navigation devices and visual devices aid reading against the linear path

Navigation tries to keep them attached to the main points and not lost readers have been disciplined into a system in which information flows into columns on a page that run top to bottom, with each line reading left to right. With the emergence of a Web screen, the specter of invoking one of Dondis's (1973) maxims—namely, "The eye prefers the lower left"—brings both aesthetic possibility and uncertainty, as it is rarely clear whether the bottom of the screen matches the bottom of the Web page.

Such differences make us suspect that visual aesthetics too differ in the two media. Certainly, as Holtzman (1998) points out, Web sites at the very least imply nonlinearity and have a discontinuity of site parts so that interactivity is required. As these structural differences play out in time, we fear that everyone who visits a Web site experiences it in a different way. (I have found many more reading patterns for printed documents than writers would like to admit as well.) If the experiences differ too greatly, we lose control over the rhetoric of the screen.

Two major types of on-line environments have been widely discussed, *experiential sites*, such as the ones built by on-line games, and *transactional sites*, such as the ones built for information exchange or commerce. These cyberspace environments, if pasted onto the continuum of aesthetics that Dondis identified, have characteristics that can be contrasted as follows:

Experiential	*Transactional*
Visual	Textual
Guided	Mapped
Movement	Still image
Wild color	Couple colors
Immersive	Interactive
Creating an experience	Revealing a logic

The experiential approach fits better with the primitive or expressionist aesthetic that Dondis articulates whereas the transactional fits better at the other end of the continuum with the functional aesthetic. Although at first glance the transactional approach to visual aesthetics seems the key for philanthropic Web site design, we need to remember that philanthropy is sometimes grounded in a bedrock of experience. That it plays off past experiences and immerses participants in creating a better place. It certainly is a question worth posing: What part does emotion play in the visual rhetoric of philanthropy sites on the Web?

Philanthropy sites on the Web

It particularizes these concerns to discuss them in relation to philanthropy sites on the Web. Thus, I turned to some prominent philanthropy sites. The larger questions—How is visual rhetoric used on the World Wide Web by sites for nonprofit fundraising? And what might we expect to develop in the ways of function, users, design sophistication, and so on?—took a backseat to discovering just what on-line presences the Web sources for philanthropy are building, both now and for the future.

My search yielded a number of fascinating entries. (See my Web page <http://omni.cc.purdue.edu/~nvo> for links to these organizations.) There is a growing on-line network for researching foundations and for supporting fundraisers with practical matters (from managing volunteers to approaching givers to crafting grant proposals). There are also directories of nonprofit organizations with pointers to their sites. So far, the Web sites are being developed by the professional organizations (particularly those with journals), foundations, nonprofit groups, and consultants. But there is little direct government involvement. The purposes seem to focus on professional contact and support. They include supporting fundraisers' efforts; distributing news and information quickly (and cheaply); connecting volunteers and organizations; increasing name recognition; and keeping information on-line. The content of these sites includes news reports, information archives, on-line discussion lists, clearinghouses for volunteers and organizations, advertisements for consulting services, and descriptive information about organizations.

Little direct information is given about the clients served by the groups—few stories, few pictures, and no audio- or videotaped messages. This may be kept from the Web by an ethical concern for the privacy and dignity of those who are served. But it is also the case that the Web is equipped to support still pictures, audio, and video. This means that the Web supports more than the logical appeals currently populating it; it also supports emotional ones.

Sites that offer advice to a group that is building a site are missing as of yet. There is little direct information about how to construct and deploy an on-line presence in a nonprofit organization (except information given by example). This is not surprising, as it is typical of the Web and even of writing not to codify strategic advice very quickly. Still, as one of the IBM Web ads suggests, everyone wants on, even if they don't have any idea why. Soon the uncertainty of purpose may change as there are growing reasons to have on-line name recognition. Take the example that much philanthropic research suggests that people give in connection with their affiliations. The Web gives organizations a presence with computer industry workers who most likely check out a group via the Web: thinking it behind the times if a group has no presence on the Web, wondering why the group is not disclosing real information if it has a slick but shallow Web site, wondering if too much money is going to advertising if the group has an expensive Web site, and so on. Thus, a Web presence may aid those groups seeking the support of computer industry workers.

As philanthropy becomes more Web-aware and groups increase their presence on-line, many issues surround on-line philanthropic discourse. The practical issues surrounding how to develop and maintain a site (particularly the technical and economic issues) normally take a front seat in a group's decision to have a Web site. Competition for funds may also well play into a group's motivation to build an on-line identity (certainly, these issues play a part in university actions and they are important in nonprofits as well). But because many of those who build and maintain the technical ends of Web sites are not trained in visual rhetoric, it makes sense for philanthropy practitioners to pay a great deal of attention to how visual and textual messages are delivered to Web visitors. Using your sensitivity to audiences is, as always, key to getting your message across.

Potential discourse issues in visual rhetoric for philanthropic discourse

The discussion so far suggests several practical questions about visual rhetoric that writers can incorporate into their writing of philanthropic discourse, as noted in Exhibit 6.1.

But these practical questions skirt the more far-reaching discussion of what issues philanthropic discourse has with regard to visual rhetoric, both in print and on-line. The issues for visual rhetoric in a print medium are clearer than those for an on-line medium. In the on-line medium we are still struggling to ask the right questions. This is true in philanthropic discourse as elsewhere.

Exhibit 6.1. Practical questions to ask about print and on-line visual rhetoric

Print	*On-Line*
Do your documents develop the look or image you want for your organization?	In what ways is it useful to portray your organization on-line?
Do the visuals represent the information needed, and do so effectively for your audience?	What kind of look or image do you want associated with your organization?
What visual rhetoric is appropriate for which philanthropy writing situations?	How do you visually emphasize the points you think important (steering visitors to these segments)?
How ought you deploy visual markers to cue your readers in this document?	How do you design an image that draws a positive with all the potential visitors (funding sources, competitor organizations, volunteers, clients)?
	How do you take advantage of the immersive potential of the Web in situations where it can aid the message you are communicating?
	How do you visually accommodate visitors with poorer connections, simpler browsers, smaller screens, and limited resources for color, animation, and visuals?

But as Charles Stephens so wisely remarked at a conference on rhetoric and fundraising: "An on-line presence must be an on-line presence as opposed to a print presence on-line. In this respect the effective nonprofit must start at the level of the established on-line visual rhetoric or all else is for naught" (1998, pp. 2–3).

To understand better and construct on-line presences for philanthropic organizations, two types of effort are needed: *From researchers* what is needed is a careful study of unfolding uses of the Web for philanthropic purposes. By examining how these sites use visual rhetoric to underscore and cue purposes and content, we will learn more about production of on-line presences in philanthropic discourses. *From practitioners* and other creative forces what is needed is the examination of how the Web can aid in the central work of your organization and the work to build an on-line presence for your group. The interesting work comes from trying to build an on-line presence that fits your group.

Through these tandem efforts, philanthropic discourse will be better equipped to understand how visual rhetoric operates into print and into Webs.

References

Barton, B. F., and Barton, M. S. "Simplicity in Visual Representation: A Semiotic Approach." *Iowa State Journal of Business and Technical Communication*, 1987, *1* (1), 9–26.

Bernhardt, S. "Seeing the Text." *College Composition and Communication*, 1986, *32*, 66–78.

Berryman, G. *Notes on Graphic Design and Visual Communication*. Los Altos, Calif.: William Kaufmann, 1984.

Bolter, J. D. *Writing Space: The Computer and the History of Literacy*. Hillsdale, N.J.: Erlbaum, 1991.

Dair, C. *Design with Type*. Toronto: University of Toronto Press, 1985. (Originally published 1967.)

Dondis, D. *A Primer of Visual Literacy*. Cambridge: MIT Press, 1973.

Felker, D. B. (ed.). *Guidelines for Document Designers*. Washington, D.C.: American Institutes for Research, 1981.

Haraway, D. J. *Modest Witness@Second Millennium. Female Man© Meets OncoMouse™*. New York: Routledge, 1997.

Hartley, J. *Designing Instructional Text*. (2nd ed.) London: Kogan Page, 1985.

Holtzman, S. *Digital Mosaics: The Aesthetics of Cyberspace*. New York: Touchstone Books, 1998.

Johnson, R. R. *User-Centered Technology.* Albany: SUNY Press, 1998.

Johnson-Eilola, J. *Nostalgic Angels: Rearticulating Hypertext Writing.* Norwood, N.J.: Ablex, 1997.

Keyes, E. Information Design: "Maximizing the Power and Potential of Electronic Publishing Equipment." *IEEE Transactions on Professional Communication, PC-30,* 1987, *1,* 32–37.

Keyes, E., Sykes, D., and Lewis, E. "Technology + Design + Research = Information Design." In E. Barrett (ed.), *Text, Context, and Hypertext.* Cambridge: MIT Press, 1988, pp. 251–264.

Landow, G. P. *Hypertext: The Convergence of Contemporary Critical Theory and Technology.* Baltimore: Johns Hopkins University Press, 1992.

Porter, J. E., and Sullivan, P. "Repetition and the Rhetoric of Visual Design." In B. Johnstone (ed.), *Repetition in Discourse: Interdisciplinary Perspectives.* Vol. 2. Norwood, N.J.: Ablex, 1994.

Redish, J. C. "Understanding Readers." In C. M. Barnum and S. Carliner (eds.), *Techniques for Technical Communicators.* New York: Macmillan, 1993.

Schriver, K. A. "Document Design from 1980–1989: Challenges That Remain." *Technical Communication,* 1989, *36* (4), 316–331.

Stephens, C. R. "A Practitioner's Response to Visual Rhetoric and Philanthropic Documents: Issues for Print and Beyond." Paper presented at the Conference on Taking Fundraising Seriously: The Language and Rhetoric of Fundraising, Indianapolis, Indiana, Aug. 1998.

Terry, J., and Calvert, M. (eds.). *Processed Lives: Gender and Technology in Everyday Life.* New York: Routledge, 1997.

Williamson, J. H. "The Grid: History, Use, and Meaning." In V. Margolin (ed.), *Design Discourse: History, Theory, Criticism.* Chicago: University of Chicago Press, 1989.

PATRICIA SULLIVAN *is director of the graduate program in rhetoric and composition and professor of English at Purdue University.*

This chapter investigates the relationship between the discourse of fundraising and corporate advertising and theorizes about the implications of the appropriation of rhetorical and linguistic devices to achieve fundraising objectives.

7

Generic patterns in fundraising discourse

Vijay K. Bhatia

ONE OF THE MOST INTERESTING aspects of discourse development in recent years has been the invasion of promotional values into most forms of discourse. Promotional genres have undoubtedly become the most versatile form of discourse. Promotional concerns have influenced the nature of the entire range of professional and even academic discourse (Bhatia, 1995). This state of affairs may be the result of several factors, including the availability of new technology for mass communication and the ensuing information explosion, the compulsive nature of advertising and promotional activities in business and other areas of social concern, and the essentially competitive nature of much of professional and academic activities.

The most significant changes we found in the 1980s were in traditional financial management areas, especially in the banking and investment sectors, which have turned advertising into a subtle art rather than the traditional hard sell. In the last few years,

NEW DIRECTIONS FOR PHILANTHROPIC FUNDRAISING, NO. 22, WINTER 1998 © JOSSEY-BASS PUBLISHERS

all advertising activities have undergone a radical change and in turn have influenced other forms of professional discourse, some of which only remotely and perhaps occasionally displayed promotional elements (Bhatia 1997a, 1997b, 1997c). Featherstone (1991) rightly claims that we are living in a consumer culture, where many of our discursive activities, whether in business, academic, or even a personal context, have to some extent been influenced by promotional concerns. The inevitable result is that many of the institutionalized genres, whether social, professional, or academic, are seen as incorporating elements of promotion. Fairclough (1993, p. 141), referring to such changes in discursive practices, points out that "there is an extensive restructuring of boundaries between orders of discourse and between discursive practices; for example, the genre of consumer advertising has been colonizing professional and public service orders of discourse on a massive scale, generating many new hybrid, partly promotional genres." He then goes on to discuss the case of the contemporary university prospectus, highlighting an increasing tendency toward marketization of the discursive practices of British universities. Apparently, academic discourse is not the only area being influenced by such mixing of genres.

The main purpose of this chapter is to analyze a range of fundraising genres in an attempt to investigate the influence of present-day corporate advertising and marketing strategies on the development of philanthropic discourse. However, before embarking on this task, it is necessary to look at some of the essential features of corporate advertising and much of promotional discourse.

Corporate advertising

Corporate advertising is perhaps the most traditional form of promotional discourse, which includes any form of nonpersonal promotion of ideas, goods, or services in order to persuade a selected group of potential buyers. Without going into a detailed generic specification of advertising genres, I summarize the optimal generic structure of the advertising genre, which seems to incorporate some or all of the rhetorical moves shown in Figure 7.1, depending on the nature of the product, the audience being targeted, and the nature of strategies used to inform and persuade that audience (Bhatia, 1997b). One may need to keep in mind that it is rare to find all of these rhetorical moves in any one advertisement and certainly not in the same order. Copywriters and advertisement designers often select from a wide range of available choices, often inventing novel uses of lexicogrammatical resources to realize some of the familiar rhetorical moves.

Product differentiation in corporate advertising

Because advertising today is so innovative and versatile, it is almost impossible to give a comprehensive account of the strategies used to influence a targeted audience. Without making any attempt to be comprehensive in this regard, I briefly take up only one strategy that has been traditionally used and that is the key concept in persuasive advertising: *product differentiation*. The copywriter must analyze all the background information, all the "evidence," in light of discovering what makes a particular product different from that of its competitors. An excellent illustration of this strategy may be found in an old story that goes somewhat like this:

In the good old days, two shops were selling sausages in the same street in London. Initially, both did well, but as days went by, the competition became tough and the promotional activities became intense. One fine morning the shop on the right side of the street put up a poster claiming, "We sell the best sausages in London." The next morning, the shop on the left side of the street, in an attempt to outsmart his competitor came up with the claim, "We sell the best sausages in England." The next day, the first shop came up with another claim: "Our sausages are the best in the world." The second shop responded, "We sell sausages to the Queen." To this, the first shop responded the following day by displaying a huge poster that read: "God save the Queen!"

Figure 7.1. Generic structure of advertisements

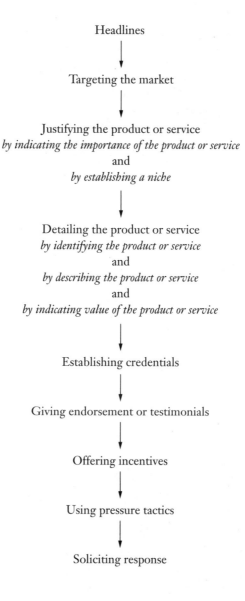

Headlines

Targeting the market

Justifying the product or service
by indicating the importance of the product or service
and
by establishing a niche

Detailing the product or service
by identifying the product or service
and
by describing the product or service
and
by indicating value of the product or service

Establishing credentials

Giving endorsement or testimonials

Offering incentives

Using pressure tactics

Soliciting response

Product differentiation is most commonly achieved by offering a product description that is good, positive, and favorable. Nowadays, the traditional practice of direct comparison of products has become somewhat risky although subtle forms of comparison are still common, as in the case of household products, where it is typically claimed that this "special" brand is much superior to an "ordinary" one. However, it is the generic values of description and evaluation that are most often called on to serve the cause of millions of products and services across the corporate world (see Bhatia, 1993, for a detailed discussion). Thus the common denominator in most product differentiation efforts is the use of the generic values of description and evaluation.

Depending on the nature of the product or service, we are sure to find interesting differences in rhetorical strategies and linguistic resources—including product description and evaluation—often leading to innovative product differentiation. Depending on how widely one casts the net, one may find a range of promotional genres in the present-day work world, some typically promotional and others not so typical, but all indicating interesting variations on the main theme. One can place a range of promotional genres in what may be called a *discourse colony of promotional genres*, which includes book and film reviews and book blurbs, job advertisements, job application and reference letters, fundraising letters and public campaigns, sales promotion letters, advertisements, grant proposals, company and travel brochures, and annual reports. Thus the colony has a variety of occupants, some with overlapping territorial claims, others markedly distinct from one another. As in any other colonial development, it is possible not only that new members are added but also that, over time, the status of certain members changes because the genre may change, develop, or become obsolete because of lack of use.

The colony's membership may also be described in terms of the degree and nature of *appropriation of promotional elements*. Primary forms are advertisements and sales promotion letters. Appropriated forms include job and scholarship applications, recommendation letters and testimonials, appeals (fundraising letters and brochures), grant and project proposals, and public documents. Misappropriated forms include political documents such as manifestos, mission statements, press communiques, and memoranda of understanding. Mixed forms include reviews (for instance, of restaurants, software, and new products such as cars), brochures (such as travel, company, and investment), leaflets (such as business, finance, hospital, and government), academic introductions (such as book forewords and blurbs), and business reports (such as annual reports and financial statements).

Fundraising discourse

Fundraising discourse represents one of the most dynamic forms of language use. On the one hand, it can be seen as a legitimate appropriation of typical corporate advertisements. On the other hand, it can be seen as one of the most dynamic illustrations of form-function correlation, second only to literary genres. It is a form of discourse in which form-function correlation is rather difficult to establish. For a relatively limited number of communicative functions, this discourse form offers a large variety of creative options, some rarely used before. It is a category of genre that offers an interesting and challenging profile of linguistic realizations to achieve a limited set of generic objectives. In fundraising discourse, we find at least five seemingly different discourse types: direct mail fundraising letters, fundraising packages for different audiences, fundraising advertisements for public participation through social events, annual reports, and grant proposals.

Fundraising discourse is essentially promotional in that it may promote a cause (as in the case of direct mail fundraising), a public campaign for social events, an image or success (as in company brochures or annual reports), or an idea or objective (as in grant proposals). We can extract various forms of fundraising discourse and place them on a continuum with many others related to promotional discourse, including advertisements of various kinds. On one end may be philanthropic purposes and on the other, commercial (corporate and individual) profit, as shown in Figure 7.2.

Figure 7.2. Commercial advertising and philanthropic fundraising

Corporate Purposes   Commercial Advertising

Product and service advertising
Goodwill advertising
Image advertising
Grant proposals
Political fundraising
Philanthropic fundraising

Community Purposes   Nonprofit Fundraising

Corporate versus philanthropic advertising

Philanthropic fundraising genres (henceforth referred to as PF) and commercial advertising genres (CA) may be grouped together in the same broad category of promotional discourse. The two genres have a remarkable degree of overlap, though one could also notice subtle differences.

Objectives

Both PF and CA primarily aim at the accumulation of capital; however, in one the main objective is the accumulation of profit for corporate purposes, whereas in the other the objective is the accumulation of funds for social welfare purposes, the basis for which is essentially nonprofit. In most cases of PF, the main driving force is the mission of the organization or fundraising agency, which is primarily used as a strategy to mobilize fundraising successfully, as illustrated in the following extract from a typical fundraising brochure: "The Black Cultural Center is a cultural treasure that enriches our community. We believe strongly that the return to the campus will be well worth your investment and ours. Please join us in building a new Black Cultural Center."

In the case of CA, however, the primary mission is to maximize profits, for either individual or corporate purposes. Even in companies where explicit mission statements are publicized, the real intention invariably is capital growth, profit enhancement, and corporate success. In the case of PF, there is always a cause for which fundraising is undertaken and that cause very often is the mission. In either case, the cause is always taken to be more important than the mission.

Motivation

The two sets of social actions (Miller, 1984), however, differ significantly in the motivating factors that make them successful. In the case of CA, the resources and expertise accessible in the form of a business proposition will convince the audience about the potential strength and eventual success of the enterprise. But in the case of PF, it is selfless motivation, social responsibility, and an urge to take moral action that will ensure the eventual success of the enterprise. In some countries, especially in the West, it is a more or less established social tradition to participate in fundraising. But I am not sure if it is entirely sociopolitical; big multinationals are also often motivated by the expectation of eventual economic advantage.

Despite these similarities in communicative purposes and use of rhetorical strategies, the two types of social action differ basically in that one (PF) is essentially viewed as a form of moral action whereas the other (CA) is seen as a business proposition. Figure 7.3 summarizes these parallels.

As indicated, a number of common features may be found in the two types of promotional discourse; however, they also display subtle characteristics that do not exactly overlap. An analysis of direct mail fundraising letters will serve to illustrate.

Fundraising letters

Like most promotional letters in business contexts (see Bhatia, 1993), fundraising letters have a relatively simple six-move discourse structure, although in practice we see only four of them used often.

Figure 7.3. Contrasts between commercial advertising and philanthropic fundraising

However, these four moves are realized through a number of strategies and each may display a wide range of linguistic resources, which makes this genre extremely versatile. The most commonly used moves and the strategies employed to realize them are as follows:

Establishing credentials

This move is often realized by one or more of the following strategies: incorporating celebrity endorsement, referring to community needs, referring to mission statements, using an image of the trustees, invoking frameworks of consciousness, and invoking community involvement.

Introducing the cause

This move often consists of the following stages: introducing the cause, describing the cause, indicating the value of the cause, indicating the potential value of solicited support, and establishing a track record.

Soliciting support

Support may be solicited through direct appeals ("Won't you join them in putting a smile on the face of a sick child?"), extended appeals ("Our ability to offer lifeline depends in large part on the generosity of a caring community, and once again, we turn to you for assistance"), and appeals with incentives ("I hope you will renew your gift of $50, and if possible, add a little more to it. The needs are greater than ever. Your tax deductible check may be made payable to the Society for the Blind and returned in the envelope provided").

Expressing gratitude

Gratitude is expressed by giving thanks for past or anticipated support, by reaffirming mission statements, and by soliciting response to the appeal.

The other two moves—offering incentives and enclosing brochures—are also used but are less common than the typical corporate promotional efforts. As we go down the list of rhetorical activity, we find increasing variation in the use of linguistic and rhetorical resources. The emerging picture seems to be the following:

Four major moves → Variety of strategies →
Wide range of linguistic realizations

Appropriating marketing and advertising techniques

Typical promotional letters begin by establishing company credentials either by referring to the needs of potential customers or by referring to the company's long-standing service record (Bhatia, 1993). In a similar manner, fundraising letters attempt to establish the needs of the members of the community, in the fulfillment of which they share an interest. This is often done by using an endorsement from a typical and credible beneficiary of the outcome of the desired action, as in the following case: "Tony is only one of the many students, staff, and faculty of all races who have sought out the BCC over the years to make new friends, enjoy the fine arts performances and lectures the BCC sponsors, and broaden their understanding of African American culture in an increasingly diverse and multicultural world. The BCC also helps Purdue departments recruit new faculty, staff, and students and supports academic excellence through its expanded library, computer lab, and outreach programs."

Community cause is often established by mission statements, as in the following claim: "The BCC is a cultural treasure that enriches our community. We believe strongly that the return to the campus will be well worth your investment and ours. Please join us in building a new Black Cultural Center."

When establishing credentials, in the case of CA a somewhat related strategy is to use a positive and long established corporate track record in providing the service or product. In the case of PF the strategy is to use the record of past successes (Bhatia, 1993): "For four years now, the Teddy Bear program has been supported by friends in the area who care" or "For nearly twenty-seven years the Black Cultural Center has served the university and the community from a small house built in 1905. If you've been there, you know the programs and services have outgrown the space. A new, much larger center is essential to carry on the mission of the BCC."

Celebrity endorsement is one of the most time-honored advertising strategies for a whole range of promotional purposes, corporate or fundraising. Notice the following attempt from a fundraising brochure: "Tony Harris, Purdue alumnus and vice president for business and customer service at Pacific Gas and Electric in San Francisco, wrote the following: 'Purdue can be a lonely place for incoming minority students. For me, the BCC represented a familiar setting, and made Purdue feel more like home.' This story I have heard repeated hundreds of times."

In fundraising discourse, this strategy is also exploited when the integrity and the public image of the trustees are used to emphasize the honest intention of the fundraising activity. It must be admitted, however, that the exploitation of the image of trustees is very subtle and indirect compared to the celebrity endorsement often used in corporate advertising.

Soliciting support

Of course, no promotional effort is complete without soliciting support, which is the main communicative purpose of the letter. It is often realized in terms of a straightforward directive: "Now it's your turn to help. If you've already made a gift or pledge, we thank you. If not, please take this opportunity to demonstrate your support by returning the enclosed form with your gift."

Like typical promotional letters, philanthropic fundraising letters also make use of enclosed supporting documents, especially forms to be filled in to pledge support and supporting brochures or leaflets. However, unlike with typical advertisements, we invariably also find the use of appeals encouraging personal involvement. In addition, we see the usual borrowings from the marketing world in the form of headlines, signature lines, and even slogans, as in the following examples: "The Center on Philanthropy—A Pillar of Community" and "Giant Steps—Toward a New Black Cultural Center at Purdue University."

Table 7.1 summarizes the essential similarities and differences in advertising and philanthropic discourse.

One of the most fundamental features of philanthropic fundraising that differentiates it from corporate advertising is the assumption that we have an interest in the establishment and maintenance of community values. Corporations are also sometimes tempted to go beyond their profit motivation to sponsor or contribute to fundraising in the hope that it will give them advantage over their competitors.

Table 7.1. Essential features of advertising and philanthropic discourse

Advertising Discourse	*Philanthropic Discourse*
Establishing credentials	Establishing credentials
By individual needs	By community needs
By long established service	By established cause
By gratitude for past support	By gratitude for past support
By celebrity endorsement	By celebrity endorsement
	By mission statements
	By credentials of trustees
	By continued community support
Introducing the offer	Introducing the cause
Offering product or service	Preparing for support
Detailing the offer	Detailing cause or service
Indicating value of offer	Value of the support
Offering incentives	Offering incentives
Special offers discounts	Income tax rebates
Enclosing brochures	Enclosing brochures
Details of offer	Brochures and mission statements
Request or order forms	Pledge or donation form
Soliciting response	Soliciting support
Using pressure tactics	* * * * *
Ending politely	Expressing gratitude

Conclusions

In this brief study I have attempted to focus on some of the interesting issues from the point of view of appropriation, adjustment, and development in genres in the context of philanthropic fundraising discourse. Specifically, I have addressed the relationship between the discourse of fundraising and corporate advertising, and the appropriation of rhetorical and linguistic devices to achieve fundraising objectives. These two specific issues then raise a more general one: the implications of this territorial invasion of fundraising discourse.

This chapter's discussion indicates that in spite of a number of rhetorical similarities between corporate advertisements and philanthropic fundraising discourse, significant factors give fundraising genres their distinctive generic integrity. Some of these follow.

Community participation. Unlike corporate advertising, which is targeted at individual customers, philanthropic fundraising values the concept of community participation. The success of the whole exercise is measured through group activity and community participation. It is considered more valuable to collect a few hundred thousand dollars from many members of the community than to collect a similar amount from a handful of rich businesspeople. As Payton, Rosso, and Tempel (1991, p. 4) rightly point out, "fundraising is . . . inextricably tied to philanthropic values, purposes, and methods." They identify fundraising as moral action, which is a major factor distinguishing philanthropic fundraising from much of corporate advertising. However, there seems to be a significant increase in the use of rhetorical strategies that are more commonly associated with the discourse of marketing, which eventually is likely to undervalue the importance of philanthropic fundraising as a community activity.

Framework of social consciousness. Schervish (1997) identifies framework of consciousness, with its own unique system of beliefs, goals, and ways of thinking and fulfilling social responsibility, as an important factor that often motivates charitable giving. Motivation for corporate success is essentially embedded within a more utilitarian framework. Any large-scale appropriation of rhetorical and linguistic resources associated with corporate advertising thus has the potential to undermine the value of even the most legitimate philanthropic fundraising cause.

Voluntary action. Although philanthropic fundraising involves large-scale community participation, it is essentially a voluntary activity. It may need persuasion, which often is in the form of tax incentives, but there is rarely a reason to use pressure tactics (Bhatia, 1993), which are so often used in corporate advertising. Even the incentives are nothing more than simple and legitimate recognition of the act of donation.

Noncompetitive stance. Promotional concerns have been at the heart of most business and professional activities and the discourse of fundraising is no exception. Although it appears to be very different from traditional corporate advertising, it shares an important characteristic: in recent years both have become extremely competitive. Just as an increasing number of new products and services are competing for favorable attention from potential buyers, so the number of fundraising activities is on the increase, as is the competition to attract contributions. In this context, it is hardly surprising that we notice an increasing appropriation of many of the rhetorical strategies and linguistic realizations that have traditionally been associated with corporate advertising. However, the two activities and hence their typical rhetorical forms remain different. As discussed earlier, product differentiation, which is one of the main underlying considerations in typical corporate advertising, is rarely an issue in most forms of philanthropic discourse.

Although many philanthropic organizations compete with one another for a limited pool of financial resources available in a particular society, this is rarely reflected in the discourse of fundraising, except in the case of grant proposals, where competition is very much at the heart of the activity itself and is reflected in the discourse as well.

As I have pointed out elsewhere (Bhatia, 1995, 1997a, 1998), it is generally less problematic to appropriate generic features across areas of discourse that serve complementary communicative purposes to create mixed or hybrid genres, as in "advertorials," "infotainment," "infomercials," and so on. It becomes more difficult to do so across genres that serve conflicting communicative purposes or that are associated with contexts that have contradictory requirements, as in the case of joint declarations, or what are more popularly known in bureaucratic contexts as *memoranda of understanding*. In such cases the appropriation of generic resources from one genre to the other often creates genres in conflict (see Bhatia, 1998). Philanthropic discourse in a number of respects appears to be similar to corporate promotional discourse. However, despite surface similarities the two areas of discourse have different underlying concerns, which may demand that they develop in slightly different directions. The real danger in an indiscriminate and overwhelming appropriation from the discourse of marketing is that it is likely to undermine the real value and strength of philanthropic discourse.

The present discussion has been based on a limited set of data from a specific cultural context, and hence the input provided may seem speculative in a number of ways. A more informed discussion of some of these issues will require a more comprehensive, rigorous, and sustained analysis of data from several other areas of fundraising and corporate advertising, as well as from a number of diverse sociocultural contexts.

References

Bhatia, V. K. *Analyzing Genre: Language Use in Professional Settings.* White Plains, N.Y.: Longman, 1993.

Bhatia, V. K. "Genre-Mixing and Professional Communication: The Case of 'Private Intentions' v. 'Socially Recognised Purposes.' In P. Bruthiaux, T. Boswood, and B. Bertha (eds.), *Explorations in English for Professional Communication.* Hong Kong: City University of Hong Kong, 1995.

Bhatia, V. K. "Genre-Mixing in Academic Introductions." *English for Specific Purposes,* 1997a, *16* (3), 181–195.

Bhatia, V. K. "Democratizing Legislative Decision Making in Hong Kong: A Study of Generic Patterns Used in Public Discourse." *Journal of Pragmatics,* 1997b, *28,* 515–532.

Bhatia, V. K. "Shifting Paradigms in Media Discourse." Paper presented at the international conference on The Three Circles of English, National University of Singapore, Singapore, Dec. 1997c.

Bhatia, V. K. "Genres in Conflict." Paper presented at the 1998 American Association of Applied Linguistics conference, Seattle, Mar. 1998.

Fairclough, N. "Critical Discourse Analysis and the Marketization of Public Discourse: The Universities." *Discourse & Society,* 1993, *4* (2), 133–168.

Featherstone, M. *Consumer Culture and Postmodernism.* Thousand Oaks, Calif.: Sage, 1991.

Miller, C. R. "Genre as Social Action." *Quarterly Journal of Speech,* 1984, *70,* 151–167.

Payton, R. L., Rosso, H. A., and Tempel, E. R. "Taking Fund Raising Seriously: An Agenda." In D. Burlingame and L. Hulse (eds.), *Taking Fund Raising Seriously: Advancing the Profession and Practice of Fund Raising.* San Francisco: Jossey-Bass, 1991.

Schervish, P. G. "What We Know and What We Need to Learn About Donor Motivation." In D. F. Burlingame (ed.), *Critical Issues in Fund Raising.* New York: Wiley, 1997.

VIJAY K. BHATIA *is professor of linguistics in the English department of the City University of Hong Kong.*

Epilogue

Ulla Connor

THE CHAPTERS IN THIS VOLUME were originally papers presented at the August 1998 symposium on fundraising and language. There, for the first time ever, linguists and rhetoricians had chosen fundraising materials as the focus for analysis. Linguists study how words and sentences are structured as systems; today many linguists, such as Deborah Tannen, also study how people communicate in real life. Tannen has studied how men and women talk differently, and how New Yorkers differ from Californians in their speech.

Rhetoricians and scholars in composition are interested in how written language appeals to the audience. Rhetoric and composition studies is a new field in U.S. English departments, greatly influenced by classical rhetoric. Thus, even rhetoricians in composition studies are examining modern-day writing; many find Aristotelian appeals helpful in explaining how writers persuade audiences. The three Aristotelian appeals are *logos* (reason), *ethos* (character of the speaker-writer), and *pathos* (emotion). A skillful persuader uses all three.

The scholars in this volume are among the best-known linguists and rhetoricians in the world, coming from as far away as Hong Kong and Tokyo. Fundraising texts were a new challenge for them. Fundraising is a perfect arena in which to study how skillful speakers and writers use language for the purpose of making relations and persuading others. Yet linguists and rhetoricians are not familiar with the specialized language use of fundraisers. Nor do they understand the context in many cases: What is a case statement? What is a capital or comprehensive campaign? What is a mission statement used for? Most of the researchers initially limited the field to direct mail letters. They first learned about the field at the planning conference in October 1997, when fifteen fundraising professionals generously and patiently explained how they felt about the field, and where linguistics and rhetoric could make a contribution to it.

Thus, the chapters in this volume are the result of this early collaboration into the directions of interest to the linguists and rhetoricians. The chapters represent a rare type of research: collaboration between scholars and practitioners to identify problems and find solutions together. From the very onset of the planning of the symposium and the birth of the original papers, there was an effort by the scholars to listen to the practitioners' suggestions about which materials to study and which questions to answer.

Naturally, one or two opportunities to interact are not enough for a new field to develop. Yet the interest that the writing of these chapters has stirred in linguistics and rhetoric is remarkable. The discourse of fundraising is accorded respect and viewed with interest by linguists and rhetoricians, along with other new areas such as doctor-patient interaction, legal language, and the language of business and industry. We who have been involved with promoting this area for study hope that it will help create a professional discourse on fundraising that brings as much pride to fundraisers as our linguistic studies of medicine and law have to doctors and lawyers.

These chapters show a promise for further study of fundraising texts by linguists and rhetoricians. Even as this volume goes to press, a large-scale study of computerized analysis of a bank of texts (also known as a *corpus*) is being implemented by a team of university researchers in cooperation with a steering committee of leading fundraising professionals. The corpus is systematically gathered from twenty-one fields in the nonprofit sector and will include case statements, annual reports, fundraising letters, and grant proposals from several agencies in every field. Quantitative analyses are planned to investigate the use of metaphors, the roles and patterns of persuasion, and even the notoriously difficult concept of effectiveness. The research into persuasion will provide us with an insight into the nature of persuasion across genres and across cultural groups. The project will result in practical advice on persuasive writing for those studying fundraising writing. This cooperation between academic researchers and practitioners is vitally important for the infusion of new ideas and techniques into the field of fundraising.

ULLA CONNOR *is professor of English and adjunct professor of women's studies and philanthropic studies at Indiana University–Purdue University, Indianapolis, where she directs the Indiana Center for Intercultural Communication.*

Index

accounting metaphor and, 43–47; more-is-up metaphor and, 41; negative connotations of, 4; nurture metaphor and, 46–47; ontological metaphor and, 42; orientational metaphor and, 41; psychic/identity rewards and, 7–8, 21; rhetorical theory and, 29; scene-act ratio and, 30–31; as scientific writing, 60; structural metaphor and, 42. *See also* Donors; Fundraising letters; Fundraising letters, content analysis of (study); On-line fundraising; Philanthropic fundraising (PF) genres; Santa Barbara (CA), fundraising in

Fundraising discourse: commercial advertising and, 101; community purpose of, 101; corporate purpose of, 101; direct mail letters and, 100; discourse types and, 100; as dynamic language use, 100; form-function correlation and, 100; fundraising advertisements and, 100; fundraising packages and, 100; nonprofit fundraising and, 101; as promotional, 100; purposes of, 100. *See also* Philanthropic discourse

Fundraising documents: creation of social roles/values and, 7; fundraising letters and, 104, 106; psychic/identity rewards and, 7–8; shame/pride and, 7. *See also* Philanthropic documents

Fundraising letters: commercial advertising and, 103; endorsements and, 105–106; establishing credentials and, 103, 105; establishing need and, 104–105; expressing gratitude and, 104; introducing the cause and, 103–105; marketing/advertising techniques and, 104–106; mission statements and, 105; offering incentives and, 104; philanthropic fundraising and, 103; six-move discourse structure of, 102–104; soliciting support and, 104, 106; supporting documents/brochures and, 104, 106

Fundraising letters, content analysis of (study): activation vs. cognition and, 32–33; advice on, 23–24; agency-agent model and, 31, 33; agent-act model and, 31, 33; altruism and, 30–31, 33; altruistic model and, 30–31, 33; argument type and, 27, 30–31; attention-need-satisfaction steps and, 32; Burke's rhetorical theory and, 29; common use of, 23; conclusions, 33–34; discourse analysis and, 25; discussion of, 29–33; Dramatistic Pentad and, 29; emotional vs. logical arguments/proofs and, 28, 32–33; empirical background and, 24–25; exchange model and, 30–31, 33; findings, 29; fundraising hypotheses and, 33–34; methodology, 24–26; Motivated Sequence and, 32, 34; patterns of arguments and, 27–28, 32; quality-need-matters-ask sequence and, 32; reliability and, 26; research questions, 24; reward-motivation and, 29–31, 33–34; sample, 25; scene-act ratio and, 30–31, 33; uniqueness of, 33; units of analysis and, 25–26

Gap, 61, 69
Genre analysis, 60
Genres: advertising, 97, 101–103; communicative purpose and, 60; customer-initiated, 63; definition of, 60; discourse community and, 60; moves and, 60; philanthropic, 101–102; promotional, 95–96, 99–100; as structured systems, 62; vendor-initiated, 63
Giving: affiliation and, 90; framework of consciousness and, 108; integrating way of life and, 8, 20; psychic/identity rewards and, 7–8, 21. *See also* Fundraising
Giving, theories of: obsession with donor motivation and, 33; reward-motivation and, 29–31, 33–34; rhetorical theory and, 29–30; scene-act ratio and, 30–31

Back Issue/Subscription Order Form

Copy or detach and send to:
Jossey-Bass Inc., Publishers, 350 Sansome Street, San Francisco, CA 94104-1342

Call or fax toll free!
Phone 888-378-2537 6AM-5PM PST; Fax 800-605-2665

Back issues: Please send me the following issues at $25 each
                 (Important: please include series initials and issue number, such as PF90)

1. PF _____

_____

_____

$ _____ Total for single issues

$ _____ Shipping charges (for single issues *only;* subscriptions are exempt
               from shipping charges): Up to $30, add $5^{50} • $30^{01}–$50, add $6^{50}
               $50^{01}–$75, add $7^{50} • $75^{01}–$100, add $9 • $100^{01}–$150, add $10
               Over $150, call for shipping charge.

Subscriptions   Please ❑ start   ❑ renew my subscription to *New Directions
                for Philanthropic Fundraising* for the year 19___ at the following
                rate:

                ❑ Individual $67   ❑ Institutional $115
                NOTE: Subscriptions are quarterly, and are for the calendar year only.
                Subscriptions begin with the spring issue of the year indicated above.
                For shipping outside the U.S., please add $25.

$ _____ Total single issues and subscriptions (CA, IN, NJ, NY and DC
               residents, add sales tax for single issues. NY and DC residents must
               include shipping charges when calculating sales tax. NY and Canadian
               residents only, add sales tax for subscriptions.)

❑ Payment enclosed (U.S. check or money order only)
❑ VISA, MC, AmEx, Discover Card #_____ Exp. date_____

Signature _____ Day phone _____
❑ Bill me (U.S. institutional orders only. Purchase order required.)
Purchase order #_____

Name _____
Address _____

_____

_____

Phone_____ E-mail _____

For more information about Jossey-Bass Publishers, visit our Web site at:
www.josseybass.com   **PRIORITY CODE = ND1**

Previous Issues Available